QUALITY
ANGLES
& The "Tantalus" Complex

Unique Perspectives On Balance & Performance ➜

RICK GRIGGS
With: MICHELLE A. CARROLL • JANICE L. EDWARDS
GREGORY R. SWARTZ • JEREMY G. WARREN
LINDA BOULDEN GORHAM

Library of Congress Cataloging-in-Publication Data

QUALITY ANGLES & THE "TANTALUS" COMPLEX
UNIQUE PERSPECTIVES ON BALANCE & PERFORMANCE
Rick Griggs ... [et al.].
          p.   cm.
          ISBN 0-922530-01-7 : $25.00
          1. Work groups.   2. Performance standards.   3. Employee empowerment.   4. Employee motivation.   I. Griggs, Rick, 1955- II. Title: Quality Angles and the "Tantalus" Complex.
HD66.Q3327   1994
658.4'036—dc20   93-38958 CIP

Printed in the United States of America

10 9 8 7 6 5 4 3 2 1

You may order this book from your bookstore. This title may also be purchased from the publisher in quantity discounts for your department or team.

For more information on the chapter authors, seminars, consulting services offered by Griggs Achievement or quantity discounts write or call:

Griggs Achievement + Manfit Press
P.O. Box 2390
San Ramon, CA 94583
510/866-0793

Dust jacket photo by Lori Roberts

Dedication

To Ed Diehl,
the quality manager and glassmaker...
you were a client, a dreamer,
but most of all,
a friend.

ACKNOWLEDGMENTS

Special thanks go to many—heartfelt gratitude to my staff, full and part time, who covered essential details during the years it took to complete Quality Angles. Sincere thanks to Shirley Xavier, Randy McClymonds, Steve Vislisel, Karen Stever, Siri Alexander Griggs, Peter Wood, and Cheryl Johanson. Certificates of endurance go to the guest chapter authors who either waited patiently while the book went through yet another year of refinement, or who were commandeered at the last minute and forced to write their chapter in a few weeks. Nice work Jeremy Warren, Janice Edwards, Greg Swartz, and Michelle Carroll. Linda Boulden Gorham is one of the most conscientious and talented workers I have ever met. Most of the outstanding Angle Views throughout the book were located, interviewed, and written by her.

Mary Diggins and Nancy Southern deserve unique mention for helping our company progress and for teaching me valuable lessons about trust, integrity, and loyalty. Finally, a meek apology to Janice Walz for the sometimes intense focus it took to produce the product you are now holding.

CONTENTS

Tantalus - A king in classical mythology who, as punishment for having offended the gods, was tortured with everlasting thirst and hunger in Hades. He stood up to his chin in water, but each time he bent to quench his thirst, the water receded. There were boughs heavy with fruit over his head, but each time he tried to pluck them, the wind blew them out of reach. (Dictionary of Cultural Literacy)

Tantalize: to torment with...the sight of something desired but out of reach; tease by arousing expectations that are repeatedly disappointed. TANTAL(US) + IZE (Websters)

PREFACE

It's hard to imagine the relationship between bullfighters, customers, stunt pilots, ski patrollers, team effectiveness, and even Classical Mythology. For nearly four years we have dealt with this connection. We went looking for a refreshing approach to work issues, personal balance, and team interaction. We found it! It is now quite difficult to imagine continuing the teaching, preaching, and cajoling that hails the virtues of perfect performance and zero defects, without looking for more of this fresh information.

Bad news—it's quite uncomfortable to hear people say they are fed up with quality. I recall hearing an employee of a major telecommunications firm say, "I'm just sick of all these quality programs, can't they just give us a break!" Good news—we intended this book to be that break from the usual. To the tired laborer, we say here's another look! To the weary team leader, we offer some unique insights. To those adding to their professional balance in all parts of life, we propose some added directions.

The original idea behind Quality Angles was to fill this volume with interesting and exciting accounts of people in unusual occupations. We would call them Angle Views and collect their personal stories about service, quality, commitment, and balance. We had a hunch that someone was out there using the information quite effectively. Interestingly, few people had ever asked them about it. The version you now hold is an adaptation where we also included interesting and useful chapters and interspersed the Angle Views among them. To spice things up further, we added an intriguing tale from the ancient Greeks and Romans.

Classical Mythology serves to guide us through the unknown and in some way, make sense of the ostensibly senseless universe we occupy. Someone, somewhere concocted a tale that would captivate and inspire, and somehow result in good. Our version of the story of King Tantalus allows today's busy and sometimes confused achiever to build a framework around productive ways to reach goals and build teams. The charm of the "Tantalus" Complex has the power to enchant and beguile at the same time. Be careful!

We introduce the term "mythical imagination" as a way to use myths to fantasize a mentor-type of relationship with the characters in Classical Mythology. If myths have been used throughout the ages for direction and instruction, can we not expand our minds and become ageless learners? Mythical imagination gives us room to have some fun and reframe our (Oops!) shortcomings and consider them "oop-tions" for 21st Century challenges.

The chapters offer an invigorating mix of experience and research. Each chapter author presents a personal view of their topic area. You'll enjoy reading about the television and broadcast industries. Listen to what Academy Award winners have to say about quality. The new model of risk taking in the leadership chapter should stimulate you to reach out and try something bold! The chapters on diversity and Total Quality offer great insights on work teams, trends in the workforce, and other vital contemporary issues. For some of you, the statistics and experimental design chapters may overreach your comfort level. Here's an opportunity where you can measurably extend your knowledge of these bottom line topics.

If by chance you encounter a chapter that takes some time to "digest" simply flip forward and treat yourself to one of the Angle Views. These "gems" will knock your socks off. They are a pure form of advice, humor, and direction. In their own flourish, these people have wonderful things for those wanting an edge for personal, career, and team issues. You won't want to miss these!

Enjoy this book. Please review what's inside from time to time and share it with others who strive for sustained accomplishment for themselves and their groups.

Good Luck from King Tantalus and myself!

Rick Griggs
Lake Tahoe (Truckee), California
March, 1994

ANGLE VIEWS

CHAPTER INVENTORIES

AUTHOR BIOGRAPHIES

MICHELLE A. CARROLL—Michelle earned her B.S. Degree in Personnel and Industrial Relations from San Francisco State University. She has spent 12 years working in the Human Resources field in companies such as Sytek, Inc., as Employment Manager, and Northern Telecom, Inc., as Human Resources Manager. Michelle currently facilitates leadership workshops and consults in Change Management and Professional Balance.

JANICE L. EDWARDS—Janice is a talk show host, actress, and television producer. She graduated cum laude from Harvard University and attended U.C. Berkeley's Graduate School of Journalism. Janice has worked for Black Entertainment Television, P.M. Magazine, KRON, KPIX, and hosts a talk show at KBHK-TV. She appears in film and performs in theatres nationwide. She served as press liaison for U.S. Congressman Ron Dellums.

LINDA BOULDEN GORHAM—Linda conducted most of the interviews featured between each chapter. She earned her B.A. in Mathematics from Montclair State College and is currently a training consultant for the Prudential Realty Group where she focuses on diversity and gender awareness & communication training. Linda has worked as a freelance writer and has designed and written newsletters for community groups and schools.

GREGORY R. SWARTZ—Gregory holds two Master's Degrees in Educational Research and Instructional Technology from the University of Oregon. He has held positions at National Semiconductor, FMC, and Raytheon Semiconductor. Gregory consults for Syntex Laboratories, National Semiconductor, Raychem Corporation, and Sun Microsystems. He teaches Total Quality Management for San Jose State University and is President of Swartz and Associates in Mountain View, CA.

JEREMY G. WARREN—Jeremy has 17 years of management experience in organizations including Corning Glass, Levi Strauss & Co., and Stanford University. He teaches a graduate course in Self-Managed Work Teams. Jeremy is President of Warren Consulting Group and Senior Associate of Ben Harrison Associates, Inc. He focuses on Change Management, Work Restructure, Empowerment, and Diversity. Jeremy received a B.S. in Psychology and an M.Ed. from the University of Pittsburgh.

The Angle on Chapter 1

*This opening
chapter brings home the idea
that the "heavy hitter" can help us
learn how to improve our batting
average in life and at work if we only ask.
The idea of sniffing out good ideas is essential
for improvement and an absolute if we are going to
have the extra time to do the things that make
life productive and enjoyable. The chapter
also introduces the "Tantalus" Complex
in the context of quality
and balance.*
RG

1

Opening Your Eyes to Quality
Rick Griggs

Wake up and smell the coffee, the roses or whatever, is good advice. When you've completed the chapters in this book and read the fascinating Angle Views, your advice to others might be wake up and ask the questions. Sniffing out good quality is like cutting expenses or losing weight. At the start, the easy items stand out like a fancy new car in an impoverished neighborhood or a logging truck to an environmental group. The low hanging fruit is easy to pick and the first few pounds are the quickest shed. Our exploration of quality in courses, lectures, books and articles shows that the first few months and years of improvement are the easiest. Some will disagree and say that getting started is more difficult than any portion of any quality or human development program. Actually they are right. When the rough and tumble start has been set in motion, that's when the quick and "easy" gains are made. After the easy ones have been knocked off is when your skill at "sniffing out" high quality performance becomes critical.

But what is quality? You're probably saying "uh oh, here we go again." Everywhere you turn and each time you read the paper or a magazine you're hit with someone's version of quality. The funny part is that each definition is good in the right setting, and each theory can benefit many industries. You've heard that quality is a good product or service. You've also been taught that quality is meeting customer expectations, a kind of customer driven process. Others say that the provider drives the customer. Witness the personal computer, VCR, some banks, and most savings and loan institutions. This thinking is that the provider invents products and services and then teaches the consumer how to use them. The masters in the field of quality teach sound fundamentals of quality including the systems approach, prevention, new ways of doing business, and team cooperation. Each of these adds value to the field. The systems provide consistency and measurement. The preventive approach is the only viable method and the only one worth rewarding. New ways of doing business means change from the top to the bottom. And it's the top that is usually most resistant to change. Finally, the cooperative approach adds a christening touch of teamwork that, if all else fails, the team can put it back together in time for customer delivery.

All of this worked well in the 1980's and well into the 1990's. Now it's time to add value, power, and application similar to the way the computer chip industry multiplies the power and speed of their computer chips. These innovative products are in your coffee maker, watch, dashboard, greeting cards, pacemakers, and doorbells. Next, we might be told when our shoes are wearing thin, the refrigerator needs cleaning, and even when there are too many fleas per square inch on the family pet. The computer industry has unleashed phenomenal power. The quality industry must do the same. The quantum leaps are not to be found in trying harder. Most companies, agencies, and individuals have already done that. Another way of thinking about quality and the definition is that it must be a fluid and changing beast. It doesn't stay the same or measure up to the same benchmarks all the time. That's how new innovations, great breakthroughs, and sizzling technologies come to market. Someone does something different. To do something different, we need some different input or stimuli. Something must make us look at the world, as if, from another planet. Or, we must take the advice of people who already look at the world, our particular industry or personal life from another surprising perspective. The next step is to bring in the heavy hitters.

THE HEAVY HITTERS

Rather than hitting baseballs out of the park, these folks aim their 300+ batting average at ideas. They hit ideas for home runs in their industry. And just like in baseball, the scouts and recruiters are scouring this country and many others to see who has that potential to smack the cowhide covered sphere out of the park in the big leagues. Well the big league is your industry or your personal life. These "out of town" players have the skills, ideas, courage, and discipline you can use, if you find it, if you understand it, and if you apply it. The truck company president has excellent ideas on teamwork, while the glass maker teaches about preparation and prevention with ease and masterful skill. Those who have professions that are one-in-the world (when you can find them) have dynamic and powerful ideas that can leverage anyone ahead even in another business, industry or family. Taking the analogy further, the real heavy hitters in big league baseball tend to strike out a lot, even sinking into month long slumps. During this time many fans begin to boo, throw things, and talk of trading the "bum" to another team. The turn around comes usually in the overall statistics where they actually produce more runs than anyone else on the team or they emerge from the slump and earn all those millions of dollars they're getting paid, much to the delight of the same fans who couldn't stomach the bad times two weeks earlier. Your search for quality angles on life will turn up experts who may happen to be in a slump, or who have been so hurt and stung by the problem times that they don't think they have anything useful to say to you. Don't believe it! They are the ones who are trying and experimenting. They will have answers.

HOW TO SNIFF FOR QUALITY

Uncovering high quality work has some great benefits. Several of the ideas and suggestions from one area will have direct application to your personal work life, and even your personal endeavors. The other gold nuggets you might sniff out will need some translation and interpretation before they will be useful to you. For example,

3

our business was advised that to be successful you had to have something to sell. The advice came from a consultant for the Federal Government during the early eighties. The person giving the advice meant having another line of business with tangible products they would sell to clients other than their main government customers. Our interpretation of that advice resulted in the addition of books and consulting products to our courses. We didn't use the information to start a sideline business but to diversify the main business we chose to pursue. This advice by the way, came from a group that is no longer in business. At the time however, they had achieved a level where they had valuable experience. My asking unleashed a flood of comments and suggestions that were, and still are useful in my business.

WHO TO ASK ABOUT SUCCESS

Spotting uncommonly good work has other nice rewards. Work that stands out may direct you to other people with answers to your quality questions. You might try asking them general questions first and later, moving on to more specific issues about what they do to perform well.

     -ask your current and prospective customers
     -ask current and potential suppliers
     -ask those making the most in the organization
     -ask those making the least in the organization
     -ask family members
     -ask people who have left the area where you work
     -ask students geared to learning
     -ask teachers geared to teaching
     -ask teachers geared to learning
     -ask anyone who is busy and productive

WHAT TO DO TO IMPROVE

Taking action in the direction of where you want to go is a great first step. In fact, no other steps matter if this one is not carried out. Be alert to the tendency for "ready-fire-aim" when it's really necessary to plan what you are going to do. Given that you have taken the time to plan what you want, how you want to get it (strategy), and who you will need to interact with, go ahead and get something done. This also means you must go, get into the elevator, car, bus, taxi or airplane and do something. A glass of action teaches as much as a pitcher of worry.

-look at the big picture without the details
-tie the details into the big picture
-walk around every day and see what's happening
-restate your purpose or mission for yourself, family, dept. agency, etc.
-list your top 3-5 priorities in any order
-rank (prioritize) the 3-5 priorities in order of importance (big picture)
-regularly change your patterns (eating, commuting, socializing, working)
-eliminate clutter and non-essentials
-eliminate a few "essentials"
-follow up immediately

WHO TO WATCH FOR QUALITY

It is tempting to attach a "successful" label to people who have lots of money, power or notoriety. These aren't always the people who have the best ideas. Your sniffing activities wouldn't be needed if the easy picks were the right picks. Take time to search and dig for people quietly doing what they do. Select from those, the ones who have risen to the top as far as skill, performance, and results. These are the only ones you want as examples. Be clear that your goal is to find transferable ideas and recommendations helpful to you, your family and your industry.

-watch anyone earning a good living
-watch people who seem calm and relaxed
-watch those who really enjoy their lifestyles
-watch anyone going about work/life in a unique or different way
-watch people who don't claim to have the answers
-tactfully gain permission to watch people who don't want you to watch them
-watch yourself
-watch your customers
-watch your family
-watch television role & leader models

WHAT TO "BE"

Most industrialized societies have molded entire populations into nations of doers, always trying to accomplish something. Maybe that's not all bad. Many of the useful and productive activities lead to great civilization builders. But instead of constantly focusing entirely on things to ask, do, and watch, here are a few suggestions on becoming the type of person or organization that gives off an air of openness and accessibility. What to be means not trying to reach an objective or open up an issue but rather setting the general tone for good information to naturally flow in your direction.

- -be open to initial distrust - they might not be used to "noisy people"
- -be relaxed taking the time to chat with people
- -be attentive while actively listening to those you're talking with
- -be a friend rather than a suspicious enemy
- -be loose and receptive to a "gray area" that's not clearly explained or described
- -be open to confusion and disarray
- -be cheerful and rested

THE HEADACHE BAROMETER

It was a marvelous sunny day in San Francisco. And I was spending the day on an island. This might make you think of the TV show "Gilligan's Island" and his stranded friends, your last vacation or your next vacation. This however was a day-long bicycle trip to Angel Island in the San Francisco Bay Area. You start by taking a ferry for $5.00. Well it's $6.00 with your bicycle but it covers the round trip fare. Aside from the beautiful scenery, great friends, and healthy exercise, we learned about Chinese Immigrants, Army operations and even a prisoner of war camp on the island. With all this, the point I remember most is buying lunch at the concession stand. I asked the young woman selling me my chicken sandwich whether or not business was good. I asked, "So how's business on a day like today?" She said, "Well I haven't got a headache yet, so it must be kind of light!"

At that moment, standing at the check stand, I would have given anything for a tape recorder and 20 minutes of her time. What would I have found out about quality, life, work, her attitudes. Has that women ever been asked about her unique "headache barometer" and how that measures good business for the day? Does someone who takes a ferry to work each day to serve chicken sandwiches to smelly bicyclists have ideas or new insights on accomplishing goals or dealing with people while working? How would she deal with rude and obnoxious customers? Or, what would she do when she gets upset, depressed or out of balance?

NOSE PROBLEMS?

Sniffing doesn't always work. Sorry, we led you this far to break the news. You probably already guessed that there might be some setbacks. I remember the executives we consulted with during the mid-eighties. These senior managers worked in high technology companies and wanted to know why employees didn't trust them. We asked the employees and the answer was they never saw them. Some of the executives took it to heart and began to take two or three walks through the area each day. Productivity took a nose-dive because the shock of this person's presence was such a change that the people couldn't figure out what was the "real reason" for the visits. As we will discuss in a later chapter on measurement, be aware that the looking around or "sniffing" as we're calling it, can create its own reaction. Try making gradual changes in your routine and be open with your motives.

READING BETWEEN THE CHAPTERS

If you're not prepared to learn, you'll think of a dozen reasons why this person's suggestion or advice is wrong. You'll also begin to show small signs of contempt as you learn more about their profession. Let's remember, these people didn't come to us to write a book, article or make a movie about the great work they are doing. These folks have been going about their business quietly and contentedly doing great work. The nose problem is not theirs. Just because no one has ever asked them for ideas, opinions, and recommendations doesn't mean they don't have shining examples of what works at home and at work. When you go sniffing for the highest quality in products, services, and lifestyles, go with an open mind and a clean...nose! The information is out there waiting for someone to come by and ask.

7

SMELL, BUT DON'T SELL FRIENDS

I remember learning a valuable lesson from an intern at a publishing conference. She had directed a question to the panel of publishers, agents and booksellers concerning the future of books with the proliferation of videos and electronic gadgetry. Her question related to the "books on tape" format. This is where they take a published book and have the author record the book on tape for those who don't have time to actually read. I forgot the panel's exact answer to her question, but I'll never forget her follow-up after they had responded. She said, "I hope you're right...nothing can replace the smell and even the feel of a good, solid book...it just wouldn't be right and I wouldn't feel the same!" Those statements, packed with vivid feelings and sentiments are a marketer's dream. In this case the issue was not the information easily available on audio cassette or in simplified form on video. She buys and reads books with an atmosphere, a tangible swirl of content, feeling, imagination, and friendship.

It reminds me of a instructor in France who cautioned our class "never sell your used books, a book is a friend and 'on ne vends pas un ami' (one does not sell a friend)!" This information was waiting for someone in the publishing industry, the tape industry or even the computer industry to simply ask the right questions of the right people.

Whether it's books as friends, computers that are friendly, or families and work groups that are balanced, someone has the answers. We run into problems when we try to tape the book, invent the new computer, and balance the family, without first digging up some information on how it's done properly. Anything can be done well, but getting it done properly is different. You can do a fine job of washing the wrong car. Office workers regularly do fine work on the wrong project. Spouses and lovers continually try something that they think will please their partner only to find that they wanted dinner instead of roses, a back rub instead of a foot rub or listening ears instead of advice. Doing the right thing well is what thousands of people around you are doing each day. You just have to find them. Many inventions were stumbled upon by accident. Someone guessed, overheard a complaint or noticed something strange like why dairy maids never contracted small pox or that excellent eye-hand coordination was needed to play video games. The first observations led to a vaccination and the second became a useful selection tool for new employees in the military and aviation.

RIGHT CHAMPAGNE...WRONG TABLE

How many times have you had the right idea, plan or party completely organized only to find you had the wrong project, date, time or location. Some people estimate that within the corporate world as much as 50% of all time and energy expended is wasted by doing the wrong things. Great work...wrong project. I once received an invitation for a Saturday evening party. When I arrived with my date the hosts were busy doing their laundry. They obviously weren't expecting company. They had changed the party to Friday, instead of Saturday, but forgot about the invitations sent out with the Saturday date. We offered to help fold!

Here's a trivial but sad story about doing the right thing wrong or the wrong thing right. It's trivial only in context of greater missed opportunities and sad because it's a tiny glimpse of how many of us have applied quality improvement concepts at work and at home. I saw a middle aged, average looking gentleman in a seafood restaurant nervously waiting for a companion. He seemed upset. I couldn't figure out why he kept going up to the bartender and asking questions. It was clear he wasn't trying to pick her up. There was chilled champagne and at least a dozen roses tastefully displayed at his table.

He was dressed in a fine suit. He lost a lot of color when he found out there was another fish restaurant several blocks away. He must have asked the waitress for directions and advice 8-9 times during the eternity of a confusing half hour. The last I saw of him he was running out of the restaurant, chilled champagne still sitting at the table, muttering something about I'll be back in a few minutes. Right setting, wrong place!

ALMOST ARRESTED...WRONG HOUSE!

It's really very easy to do the right thing wrong or the wrong thing right. In my life, it results from not getting enough information from the right people, Here's a funny situation that could have gone terribly wrong had it been in another neighborhood. While doing a friend a favor I thought I was going to get arrested. He needed to borrow my truck to move a couch. I said sure, although I couldn't go with him we would trade vehicles after I helped load the couch into my Jeep. Just after 5 pm I drove down his street looking for his house. I saw his car parked in the street near an open garage door. I drove past, put it in reverse and backed into the garage. I walked into the patio, called his name and looked into the window, but it didn't look like his furniture. Suddenly, I realized I was at the wrong house and imagined police would probably be arriving to get me at anytime. He lived next door but had parked his car one house away to make room.

Good sniffing should get you and the champagne to the correct restaurant and avoid any close calls with police officers. These examples are indicators of what goes on everyday at work, home and around the community. By not finding the right people and not asking the right questions we have little chance of making better than average progress towards where we wish to go. If an agency wants to improve morale or decrease expenses, the leader can do the usual routine and try real hard to make it happen. Another option is to go outside of the agency, and even the industry and sniff out what other people are doing with similar issues or even different issues. If you look at similar issues you'll get directly transferable ideas. When you examine other issues in outside areas what you'll find will be new or unique methods of getting tasks accomplished or ideas implemented. For example, one family might look at other families and other issues. Perhaps the other family has a teenager with dating and school problems combined. Their method of pulling together and solving the problem might include evening discussion, family brunches each Sunday, and a family suggestion box. Our family doing the sniffing might apply these ideas to the vacation issue. They benefit from the new perspective and the new methods of settling issues. Good searching and sniffing help you avoid a frightening complex discussed below.

THE "TANTALUS" COMPLEX

King Tantalus was a figure in classical mythology who had offended the gods. You'll remember that these gods especially Zeus, the god of gods, had horrible tempers. They turned people into half-beast half-men, chained them to rocks, had their livers eaten, and cast them into the labyrinths to die of starvation and exhaustion. And all this while hurling thunderbolts, fighting the Trojan war, and chasing mortal women. Classical mythology is filled with Greek and Roman stories of valor, lust, victory, defeat, and punishment. This is where we get sayings such as "beware of Greeks bearing gifts," Alexander the Great's "cutting the Gordian knot," and being caught between "Scylla and Charybdis."

Well, this brings us to King Tantalus. His offense to the gods condemned him to everlasting torture in that most dreadful place called Hades. Today we call it hell. Rather than roasting or being torn apart by starving beasts, his torment was specifically aimed at his hunger and thirst. He remained up to his chin in water but each time he bent to drink the water receded. The trees above him were full of ripened fruit, but each time he reached up, a sudden gust of wind blew them out of reach. Each and every effort made by King Tantalus was met with a contradictory event that nullified the attempt. The "Tantalus" Complex is born!

TOWARDS AND AWAY FROM GOALS

The essence of the "Tantalus" Complex is that, like King Tantalus, each of us as individuals, and each of our organizations does contradictory things that take us five steps towards our quality levels and then five steps back. Without purposely trying to sabotage our efforts, we perform one task that moves us forward and another that moves us backward. The company teaches prevention and then rewards crisis management, the bicyclist rides for health and yet, doesn't wear a helmet, and the politician raises adequate funds, but consorts with the wrong people. All of these are examples of working towards and away at the same time, the heart of the King Tantalus predicament.

Here's a bit of preview information on the three levels of the complex. Take a look at them now to help underscore the need to dig out accurate and useful information that takes you towards rather than away from your goals.

Level 1—minor contradictions: These are little things that will always be challenging for anyone doing several things at work or in life. They cause the little nuisances and headaches but we are the only ones to blame. We lose up to 10% of our effort around these level 1 issues.

11

Level 2—major contradictions: This is starting to get serious. This is the point where we are negating a lot of our effort and energy by spinning our wheels or undoing a large portion of what we have already built. The loss amounts to 10-30% or our energy being wasted.

Level 3—tragic contradictions: Finally, the third level of the "Tantalus" Complex is where a major portion (over 30%) of life and work is allowed to evaporate because of the contradictory patterns, and a somewhat unconscious way of living and working. The person at this level affects himself/herself without a doubt, but they rarely notice it until it has hurt others.

"TANTALIZING" THINGS TO COME

There's more to say about the "Tantalus" Complex and how it fits into the picture of achievement. Your work and your personal life may have many examples of this complex. You'll notice it whenever a person or a group works towards goals and works away from them at the same time. The definition of "tantalizing" is something that a person wants badly but cannot get. Well, you will get more on this eye opening subject and how it might be affecting your life. The final chapter (Ch. 10) will continue our discussion of the "Tantalus" Complex, obsessed and possessed forms of achieving, and something called "mythical imagination." For now, keep in mind that good "sniffing" and honest feedback can keep you, your family, and your team away from the harmful levels of this "complex" and still let you build onto your dreams.

Well, you may not have another definition of quality to add to the list, but we hope you'll have a different way of looking at it. Is it that important that your definition of quality includes customer expectations, prevention, systems approaches, zero defects, and management upheaval? Maybe it needs some or all of these. We hope that as you continue through this book, you'll find other valuable tools and stimulating perspectives to sustain you in your effort to reach personal and team goals.

The Angle Views you will find interspersed between the chapters of this book should highlight the importance of mixing superb information with new perspectives. They might even have a few insights for avoiding the "Tantalus" Complex. Just like in the classical myth, it's foolish to move towards your goals and away at the same time. Good information and new perspectives will lead to quality products, services, and even lifestyles.

POINTS TO REMEMBER/THINGS TO DO

1. Look to other industries and professions for useful ideas.
2. Ask productive people what they do and how they do it.
3. "Sniff" around for high quality in services and products.
4. Watch clues leading to new, useful ways of doing things.
5. Plan for time to carefully read the rest of this book.
6. Recognize the 3 levels of the "Tantalus" Complex. Pick your battles carefully.
7. Focus on improving one specific area of "Tantalus" in your life.
8. Take a peek at the final chapter for more on King Tantalus.

Team Values, Culture & Beliefs

Here is one group's attempt to "open their eyes" by refining values. These solidify the culture and beliefs of a team and give individual members "guide posts" for calibrating their activities.

WE VALUE CUSTOMER SERVICE—as the overall reason for existence in the business world. This value builds and then maintains mutually beneficial relationships. Our customers and clients go to the top of all priority scheduling and "to-do" lists.

WE VALUE SERVICE TO SOCIETY—We exist to make positive changes for humankind. Our intent is to change the world in a permanent and valuable way. Our courses, consulting, books, and products show that balance and achievement are not only added together, but multiplied for a return to society many times greater than their individual worth.

WE VALUE BALANCE—in all areas of a person's life. We define balance as a "stable, calm state of the emotions—a satisfying arrangement marked by even distribution of elements...characterized by the display of symmetry." Balance is not always achieved but constantly aimed for.

WE VALUE INTEGRITY—in the large and small areas of life. This is an on-going effort to integrate our professional philosophy and remove any false masks, pretensions or impressions. Integrity means doing the right thing when no one else will ever know.

WE VALUE GUTSY COMMITMENT—which seems to be a combination of raw courage, clear insight, and perseverance. This implies an understanding and execution of systems and processes that, if followed with discipline, will lead to goal accomplishment.

WE VALUE UNDERSTATEMENT—We believe in under promising and over delivering. This is vital for building strong, on-going relationships. Our reputation will be built on quality of work, which speaks for itself, rather than quick fix compromises. Understatement is compatible with our company beliefs in relationship building and in long term balanced achievement.

WE VALUE PERFORMANCE, INITIATIVE & LOYALTY—as the standards expected of our people. We value these three success ingredients even more highly when they are combined with unselfish teamwork to achieve long term, balanced relationships among ourselves and our clients. In other words, we reward people who get results, take responsibility, and protect the organization.

14

Team Values Worksheet

Values: "Ideals, customs, institutions etc., of a society {group} toward which the people of a group have an affective regard. These values may be positive, as cleanliness, freedom, education...any object or quality desirable as a means or as an end in itself." (Websters)

We value

_____
_____
_____

We value

_____
_____
_____

We value

_____
_____
_____

We value

_____
_____
_____

We value

_____
_____
_____

We value

_____
_____
_____

We value

_____
_____
_____

(Permission granted to copy this form after purchase of book)

Angle View 1
AVALANCHE!
Mark - Ski Patrol Director

"Average doesn't work for me," said Mark. Outstanding performers on any team have a real dedication, a personal pride in what they do. They understand that how they perform goes beyond just one act, but sets a tone for the entire group."

Mark is director of ski patrol for a large snow ski resort that was the site of the 1960 Winter Olympics. He directs the activities of between 30 and 40 regular ski patrollers, up to 40 additional part-time patrollers, and a staff of eight. To be on his team, skiers must have a combination of technical and interpersonal skills. He likens the requirements to that of firefighters.

"Everybody who skis doesn't interact with the ski patrol. In fact, probably very few do. But for the people who do, I want that interaction to be a very positive experience. I want my staff to be competent, efficient, friendly, and attentive to both the medical and emotional needs of the visitors. Fortunately, in most cases, that's the kind of people I have working for me."

Anyone who ever had the image of a patroller as a ski bum is on the wrong track. Mark said where that may have been accurate at one time, it clearly doesn't apply anymore. It is a very demanding profession, doesn't pay well, and requires sophisticated and diverse skills. Mark should know, he started as a patroller. His previous experience combined with his enthusiasm for the job earned him early promotions. After only three years he was promoted to director. As director his duties are to implement the policies designed to enhance the safety and enjoyment of the ski area for the customers and staff. In addition to general management, he is also responsible for training the staff and directing the hill marking and avalanche control operations.

For Mark, a high quality performance requires a thorough knowledge of the job. Also, the performer who stands out as exceptional, pays attention to details which, in his business, could mean the difference between life and death or at least safety versus danger. Then there's an extra component that clearly separates the good from the superior. Says Mark, "Your job should have some sort of special meaning for you. You should put in your creative flair and personal touches

Mark's personal touch is to provide an atmosphere that has as much support as possible. "People always want to be associated with a successful, well thought of team. People produce when they feel pride in what they do. I try to foster that as well as their own feeling of empowerment. I think most people appreciate the effort I put into being the manager of the ski patrol. Yet there's only so much I can do. I can't really pay people what I'd like to pay them. They understand that my expectations are very high. I'm going to have the same expectations no matter what I'm allowed to pay people. So I try to have the best work environment that I can give in those particular constraints. People appreciate that. They appreciate me.

As Mark said, low salaries come with the patroller's job. There's also the beauty of being on a mountain of new snow at dawn, the flexibility of having a seasonal work schedule, and the exhilaration of seeing the beauty and power of the avalanches they purposely set off before skiers arrive to ensure the safety of the resort. Add to that the tremendous sense of value and pride they get in being able to rescue people in distress and/or attend to their medical needs.

"My previous boss never let anybody do anything. That's the exact opposite of the way I feel. My feeling is if you want people to not do quality work, you do everything for them or always be critical because they didn't do it your way. To be rigid and always do things that you've hired others to do is the most effective way to limit people's initiative and the quality of the work they're going to produce. The less I do, the better I'm doing my job."

Doing a good job also means having a balanced life. "Balance means absolutely everything to me. There was a time when my work defined everything about who I was or at least that's the way I felt. I had the great fortune to meet a wonderful woman who allowed me to see some of that balance. Now my complete focus is not on work. I've tailored my working schedule so I only work seasonally and have three months off. I need the break because in the winter it's not unusual for me to put in 60-70 hours a week several times during the ski season. I have a lot of other interests. If that was constrained, I'd really have to consider changing what I was doing. Changing work, not changing my life."

Angle View 2
LOVE, HEADACHES & WEDDINGS
Claudine - Owner/manager wedding facility

In love? Getting married? Well, you may want to start your planning by making a trip to the sneaker store and buying a good pair of running shoes. Now, put them on and start running. Go to the bridal salon, tuxedo rental, bakery, travel agency, shoe store, limousine rental and the florist. Don't forget the caterer, church, local hotel, reception hall and photographer. Tired? Here's another idea. In the San Francisco East Bay there is a complete one-stop wedding facility where everything can be taken care of under one roof. Everything!

Opened in 1991 and owned by Claudine and Bob, this facility is only one of four in the United States that can completely satisfy a couple's wedding needs. Claudine gave some comments on how she and her husband got the idea to build the facility and how quality management became part of their philosophy.

"My stepson who lived in Utah called us a while back to say he was getting married and asked us to come down. Well, the couple hadn't done much planning and my husband ended up running around town for a week with his soon-to-be daughter-in-law trying to get everything they needed to quickly put a wedding together. After that experience, which my husband declared a 'headache,' we found a place in Utah which provided an all-in-one facility. We thought the idea was a good one and felt there was a need for a similar facility in other parts of the country. When we returned home we bought 10 acres and proceeded to build this complex specifically for that purpose."

"In the planning and construction phase we paid attention to some quality details that we feel are unique. The church windows were positioned and selected to accommodate the needs of our photographers and video experts. In addition, the type of glass was designed to eliminate glare and yellowing in pictures. The outdoor wedding pavilion was cut into a hillside to provide an appropriate backdrop for pictures and was placed to avoid the intense rays of the hot sun. Upstairs in the bridal shop and tuxedo rental areas, the lighting and mirrors were specifically selected and positioned for the best effect."

One of the key areas of concern for Claudine as manager is time. She said, "For me it is critical that everything be on time. That's quality for our operation. I want the staff to work on time, the events to be ready to start on time, and the food prepared in a timely fashion." "In fact," she continued, "I can remember one wedding where time was critical in an unusual way. The bride wanted to put a time one hour earlier than the actual wedding time on the invitation. She was convinced her family would not be on time. I felt uncomfortable with that because I felt the conscientious guests would probably arrive up to a half hour early and as a result would have to wait an hour and a half. We compromised. We put the proper time on the invitation and included a special note about the importance of being on time. When the day arrived there were only five guests on time. We had to delay the wedding a half-hour."

It just goes to show that in Claudine's business, each wedding will have its own personality. Claudine feels she has been successful in really listening to the concerns of her brides and grooms. Sometimes, she says, they know what they want; other times not at all. But she feels that by taking the time to ask questions, she is able to ascertain what couples want to make their day special. Once that meant sitting with a bride until 1:30 in the morning.

Claudine added, "I have to be prepared for anything. Once after a ceremony when the first dance was ready to begin, the bride started singing to her new husband. Nobody knew of her plan (except perhaps the band). My staff, the guests, and of course the groom were all surprised. But she had a beautiful voice and it worked well. Although unexpected, that was tame compared to the plans for an upcoming event. The bride plans to do a belly dance after the ceremony. At least I'll be prepared for that one."

Some see
it quite clearly. Others are
blind to the value of sanctioning qualified
people to carry the banner forward. The power
that a leader vests in others can be multiplied and
expanded into great results. This chapter peeks around
the "corner" at five empowerment case studies. Each has
a direct and lasting effect on individual performance
and self-esteem. Take a look at some
interesting ideas on how to
empower your team.
RG

2

HOW TO EMPOWER A TEAM
5 case studies
Rick Griggs

Empowerment requires trusting relationships. Responsibility can be delegated to trained people with authority and motivation to act in the best interest of the organization. Empowerment breaks down when one or more pieces of the puzzle are missing. These pieces of the puzzle are evolving in various industries but they often include things like the tools needed, the training, communication, clear vision and direction, and powerful trust in those being asked to perform.

I think back on my days in Little League baseball when my brother and I often played on the same teams with varying coaches year after year. One year after a great season, my brother and I made the all-star team. My brother being a better ball player, usually made the team. However it was my first time, and I got to experience a sudden change in coaches and coaching style. I felt confident and trusted with my regular coach. The new all-star coach somehow made me feel pressured and less confident in my fielding and hitting skills. To this day I remember a nervous at-bat where instead of swinging hard, I simply tried not to strike out or do something stupid. I grounded into a double-play when I know I could have done much better. I lived up to the exact level of empowerment given to me by the coach. We also lost the game.

The following cases will highlight some good and bad examples of individual leaders and organizations making attempts to empower others in order to get the agency's work accomplished. Some cases will contain both good and bad aspects, and you will be challenged to separate what works and what doesn't. Like a good coach, some leaders know how to invigorate others, while some struggle with less effective methods.

Case 1: THE PART-TIME LEADER

Patrick was brought in as a part-time manager of an owners' association for a large industrial business park. His other duties were varied and complex, yet he added this job to the list. Karen was in the role of office manager and marketing coordinator. She saw the need to survey the property owners and hire a consultant to work with the team to train and develop them around missions and objectives that would meet the needs of the owners. At the same time she hoped an added benefit would be some nice team building among the staff.

She went to Patrick with the idea and got approval to begin the process. Patrick not only gave her the authority and flexibility but, on her request, attended the vendor selection meetings and gave critical input on the desired outcomes. The vendor remarked that his input and involvement in no way overshadowed Karen's efforts but instead molded with them and gave the impression of a flexible, cohesive team.

Patrick offered a few ideas of his own for presentation during the series of courses. He did it in a way that showed interest in the success of the trainings and excitement about the new concepts. He did not force the issue but waited patiently until it fit into the flow of the unfolding sessions.

21

Although Karen managed the process and logistics, Patrick attended each session and participated in a moderate and smooth fashion. He never used his position of power to force ideas or to garner support for ideas or comments he would make. The group made independent decisions with him in the room. These were good decisions that led the way for meeting more of the stated objectives of the agency.

CASE 1 ANALYSIS: Patrick's style worked partially because he had a qualified and motivated employee to start with. Karen took complete ownership of the project and treated it with the care and attention it deserved. This did not occur spontaneously but after several instances where she took initiative and her boss allowed increasing levels of autonomy and control. The trust and empowerment may have begun as a tentative experiment. In any case, it grew into a useful and effective tool that benefited everyone on the team. Any boss's challenge would now be to replicate this good result with as many on the team as possible.

Case 2: IT'S YOUR NEWSLETTER

Ed managed the quality department for a computer manufacturing firm. After the entire management staff went through an introductory quality awareness program they still noticed some rough edges within and between departments. Everyone knew that the one training session wouldn't solve every problem, but they were a bit dismayed at the extent of what persisted.

The president authorized a comprehensive assessment of over 20 groups within the organization using a problem solving and decision making tool called Profile-Scans. The resulting consensus formed around the lack of communication. It didn't end there. Most groups agreed that an ideal method to solve the problem would be to start a company newsletter. Ed's department was nominated and Becky, the department secretary, was given the responsibility for getting it done.

Ed wanted and insisted that it succeed without many glitches since all other departments were looking on to see if this effort at another newsletter would be any better than the ones tried in past years. Ed empowered Becky by giving her the responsibility along with the authority to succeed. He stayed involved but made it clear that it would be under her direction. In essence, he turned the flow of power and authority upside down in his relationship with Becky.

The newsletter was a hit. It achieved the goal of plugging many of the communication holes that were plaguing the firm. She added quality awards, letters to the editor, a message from the president, and articles from previously "unknown" departments and product teams. Although they later switched from monthly to a quarterly format, it expanded over the years in pages and coverage. Many groups ordered extra copies to be routinely delivered to key customer accounts.

No one knows for sure if Becky's go-getter personality would have been enough to do the job or if Ed's skill in setting up the right environment was the key factor. Maybe it's a combination of the right amount of empowerment, at the right time, to the right person or team.

CASE 2 ANALYSIS: Here again, the manager's style worked and meshed well with a ready and willing employee. We can begin to entertain the thought that rather than style, the manager is demonstrating a superior level of patience and skill. In most cases, it takes a bit of grooming to have several employees like Becky in a single department. Similar to the patience required to delegate, empowerment grows when the leader takes small and consistent steps toward giving up power and authority. The process is scary to most but the results are quite promising.

Case 3: THE "TOUGH GUY" BOSS

Rudy was on the fast track at a semiconductor manufacturing company in Silicon Valley, California. He hadn't quite finished his master's at a Northern California University, but he landed the job anyway. He quickly established himself as a fast learner and a risk taker. He worked hard, including evenings and weekends, and won a promotion to start the company's productivity department.

With the blessing of the president, Rudy rushed to bring in fresh talent from his alma mater. He selected people who would appreciate the pay and thus, work "till they dropped." Stephanie was one of his first hires. She performed above his expectations and began to get outside recognition and credit that seemed to bother

Rudy. He remarked that they needed to remove the "halo" from one of her stellar projects so she wouldn't get overconfident. Stephanie started to notice certain projects and vital information were being given to other members of the department in a competitive manner that made all of them keep secrets and jealously guard information.

Stephanie struggled with what she saw emerging. They had gone to graduate school together and genuinely respected each other. Now their friendship and the working relationship were starting to diverge. Instead of leveraging the stable friendship into a productive work situation Rudy seemed to deflate most of what she tried to accomplish. The friendship glossed over all the early stages of anger and disbelief.

One of the final straws that convinced Stephanie to consider recruitment offers from other companies was the time Rudy came up to her while she was talking to a few friends and co-workers. He said in a solemn, somewhat stern voice "I'd like to see you in my office...now!" Stephanie felt embarrassed and even deflated at the way he did this in front of her peers. She immediately followed him into his office only to find he had nothing to discuss but only wanted to chat. She interpreted the scenario as a power play intended to lower her standing in the group. Soon after, she accepted an unsolicited offer from a competitor to manage an entire department. It included a 10% pay raise and a certain number of free shares of company stock for each of the first four years.

CASE 3 ANALYSIS: Rudy was an insecure and inexperienced manager. He feared the level of accomplishment one of his direct reports might attain if she continued her excellent performance. Although he saw areas of legitimate improvement, he could not engage in healthy dialogue without ridicule and game-playing. He saw her success as a threat to his superhero status rather than a stellar addition to the team. His actions would eventually lead to mediocre performance by the majority of his team members.

Case 4: THE NEW TRAINING MANAGER

This case occurred in the high technology industry during the boom times of the early 80's. This 15 year old firm had become one of the co-leaders in the industry. Most employees felt it was a privilege to be employed by an industry leader. The lower pay scale was balanced by the prestige and job security. The company had a plant manager who reported to a division manager. Within the plant there were production, engineering, research and development, and training managers.

Jim was brought in to be the new training manager. This was a position upgrade. The previous person in the position had been a supervisor. He would start with a two-shift operation, with two supervisors and progress to a three-shift operation, with an additional shift supervisor. The total department staff, including trainers, was about 30.

This was an ideal situation for someone willing and able to dedicate his career and daily energy to making the department work well. Jim had waited for this type of opportunity and planned to do all he could to make his mark on the organization and be a great boss to the people he would manage.

During the first week on the job Jim was asked to present a strategic plan for the department. In the middle of the presentation two of the engineering supervisors and one from production heckled and berated Jim for the previous actions of the department. Jim was shocked at the sudden rude treatment and explained that he had just come aboard and that the department had been without a leader for several weeks since the previous supervisor had left. He was told that this was a no-nonsense company and that accountability was exact. But he asked, how could he have "anything to do with what happened before he arrived?"

Jim thought carefully as he made his concluding remarks taking careful note of the plant manager's non-involvement in neither the accusations nor his defense. The same person who had cheerfully interviewed him, called him at home, and genuinely encouraged him to take the company's offer sat there and let a group of unhappy managers and supervisors vent their frustrations on a new person during their first week in a new job.

He began the job not knowing whom to trust and whom to watch with an eagle eye. Jim started the job with a grating sense that blame and finger pointing would be common. He wondered if he had made a mistake.

CASE 4 ANALYSIS: This unfortunate initiation would take the wind out of many sails. Some people respond to provocation with increased energy and more hours on the job but real empowerment can't flourish in this setting. Worse yet, the person responsible for the entire plant lost an opportunity to develop trust and show fairness by example. His future efforts to empower, if any, will be looked at with suspicion and hostility. The manager may have abdicated his position to empower and will likely have to rely on threats of coercion and security around money to motivate his staff.

Case 5: JOE SETS THE EXAMPLE

Joe founded a successful start-up company with two of his old friends. Down the road, a larger firm purchased the company and made it a wholly-owned subsidiary. This meant that it belonged to the larger firm but maintained much of its autonomy, products, and client base. Joe remained president and the others retained their positions as vice-presidents of sales and marketing, respectively. Over time, their success gradually began to slip. Joe took the advice of one of his senior engineers and contracted with a consultant to work with his team to upgrade their overall mission and strategic plan.

From the start, Joe showed signs of complete support and trust in the employee who had suggested the process. He examined the consultant finalists, interviewed them, and ultimately followed the engineer's original recommendation on the best person for the job. He also listened to staff members' and the consultant's advice on the general content for the working sessions. Joe made it a point to have the class reading done ahead of time so he could encourage other staff members to complete all details of the program.

Of particular interest was one assignment where each department head had to clearly define the mission of their area and the attendant success factors or major objectives that would support the mission. Joe knew that he had top notch personnel who would take the initiative and run with it. He arranged to have his portion done and reproduced in advance so that each could connect their activities to the big picture. He knew that his completed mission and success factors would be the basis for a large part of each department head's assignment.

This may not seem unusual on the surface, but many leaders have trouble admitting that they have not already hammered out and delivered these same materials to all direct reports. Sure, it's covered at staff meetings and other sessions, but to really re-think the values and the mission and open it to critique and individual interpretation requires considerable courage and insight.

The organization regained its momentum and continued to do well. Joe had to cancel a follow-up session nine months later because he had been promoted to executive vice-president for the parent company. His key staff members were also promoted into corporate vice-president positions. Something he was doing was especially effective and the chairman of the board noticed it.

CASE 5 ANALYSIS: Joe put pretensions aside and did what was needed for his team to make progress. His staff didn't have to watch their backs or react defensively to a barrage of accusations or threats. Joe demonstrated an ability to be open and vulnerable, yet highly capable. His staff saw where they fit in and how much they were needed to make the team function properly. He didn't have to beg and plead—he empowered them and let them perform.

POINTS TO REMEMBER/THINGS TO DO

1. Methods of empowering people can differ by job type or industry.
2. Trust is a major component of empowerment.
3. People know when the leader is insecure and cannot delegate.
4. Try giving more flexibility to others in order to stretch your comfort zone.
5. Never assume you can do the job better than your team or department. If it's true then train and develop them.
6. An empowering manager or workplace is worth money to many employees.
7. The rules are always changing. Keep up with them to avoid Tantalus.
8. When you apply empowerment well, it works marvelously.

Customer Satisfaction Inventory

You can't empower your team in a vacuum. Any team needs clear guidance to be able to feel confident as they test their new powers. Develop an inventory with their support. Post it. Follow it.

1. Our primary customers are internal co-workers, external clients or a mixed combination of the two;
    ANSWER =

2. We clearly communicate to ourselves and others who our main customers are on a weekly, monthly, annual basis;
    ANSWER =

3. We talk with our customers daily, weekly, monthly;
    ANSWER =

4. We visit our customer locations weekly, monthly, annually;
    ANSWER =

5. We select and apply the correct standards to match what our customers want, need, and expect;
    ANSWER =

6. We don't trust last year's assumptions, or even last month's...things continually change. We review assumptions weekly, monthly, quarterly;
    ANSWER =

7. We acknowledge and reward the preventive efforts made by balanced and well-rounded people on our team;
    ANSWER =

8. Our customers view us as a benefit toward reaching their goals;
    ANSWER =

9. Customers have at least three (3) ways to give us feedback;
    ANSWER =

10. We seek out information even from complainers and dissatisfied clients;
    ANSWER =

(Permission granted to copy this form after purchase of book)

28

Angle View 3
TO CATCH A THIEF...& CURE CORPORATE CANCER!
Mark - District Manager, retail store

Mark is a district manager in charge of 13 stores that form the southwestern operation of a large specialty retailer. In five years with the company, Mark has risen quickly, and developed a great deal of enthusiasm for the company, its potential, and its people. The "pride in perfection" attitude for the company mirrors Mark's personal goals for himself.

"I am an individual who believes very strongly in the strength and quality of what you do and what you believe in. I believe in having a tremendous amount of enthusiasm in your job and being willing to stand up and be noticed. Also, everything I do is done to make this company more successful. If anything has characterized my stay with this company, it is that I most definitely provided commitment and enthusiasm."

Mark's responsibilities run the gamut from sales, personnel, inventory control and budgeting, to advertising and marketing. He sets high standards for his stores and for himself. Said Mark, "The quality of my work is based on the success of each individual location, the maturation of the management staff for each store, and my ability to maintain and enhance the standards of this company. The managers report to me on a daily basis. I reflect on what they do based on their performances, how well they listen to my leadership, and how well they follow the policies that I extend out to them. Their rise through the company and personal improvement are a reflection of how well I am doing. Watching them reach goals is something I personally take pride in as they mature through the company. In addition to their success, my personal satisfaction is based on the feedback I get from corporate headquarters as well as our customers."

For Mark, one of the keys to having successful managers is hiring people who are intelligent, driven and eager to move within the company. "I as a manager like to surround myself with people who are willing to place themselves in a position where they see themselves progressing, and are willing to make daily strides to get ahead. Most managers fail because they fear hiring or promoting people who are better than they are. It is a cancer to companies.

29

"I think (to alter the phrase) every great person has one or two great people behind him or her that make that person successful. Too many times people try to take things on their own. I just don't think that can be done."

In addition to his staff, Mark attributes that philosophy to his family and his friends. "You have to have people in your personal life that respect and understand what you do." Mark continued, "They have to be able to understand that there will be times when things will go out of balance, and they have to be somewhat resilient to those times. I have experienced both ends of the balance issue. You are never going to be able to balance your life on a day-in, day-out basis. You're going to have swings that go both ways. What's important is essentially knowing how far you're going to allow yourself to swing one way or the other. At 35, I've been through a marriage, have a son, and have had things happen to me personally that threw that balance out of whack. But I've always been blessed with family members, friends, and now my new wife who have been absolutely, phenomenally supportive."

On the issue of problems, Mark feels the quality of a manager is not in how many problems he incurs, but how successfully he's able to move around or through them. One of the most disheartening type of problem for Mark is when managers disappoint him because of their actions. "I've had to have probably 8-10 managers arrested for stealing (remember Marks works for a specialty retailer). Now these were people I had put a lot of time into and worked very closely with. To watch somebody mature through the company and allow themselves to be influenced by whatever, to the extent they put their job at risk, is a real disappointment to me. I feel very badly about that."

Aside from the obvious recommendation (don't steal!), Mark has some suggestions. "Establish realistic goals. I feel there are no such things as unrealistic goals, just unrealistic time frames. Once you set your goals, pursue them daily. Be focused and be willing to listen and pay attention to what's going on around you. No one is so self-confident that they can't listen. That is the short-coming of a lot of people."

Angle View 4
PARIS, A ROLLS-ROYCE & THE SAUDIS
Ted - Executive, national insurance company

Ted is an executive with a national insurance company. In his twenty-year tenure he has risen from an appraiser to a top position in the company's real estate subsidiary. Ted directs 25% of the company's value of over 6 billion dollars. His responsibilities are to direct the leasing, managing, developing and selling of the diverse commercial real estate holdings.

At Ted's level of authority, doing a good job is largely based upon his ability to motivate and empower the dozens of management personnel in his east coast home office as well as several regional office locations. One of the attributes that has contributed to his rise in the company has been his ability to know and appreciate his staff's strengths and weaknesses.

"I've found that when you put a group of people together, each of them will have an individual talent where they'll really shine and do better than others. If you can select a project and then put the people in it that have the right skills, you can really get the job done."

Getting the job done with and through people is part of Ted's management style. In addition to trying to put the most effective teams together, quality management for Ted involves autonomy and empowerment. "We generally set goals for ourselves during the year. I try to make sure they are clear, quantifiable and realistic. Usually management wants us to try to get more than we think we can get, so goal setting frequently requires some negotiation. The way we meet and/or exceed these goals helps determine how successful we've been all year.

"Once the objectives are set, I delegate the total responsibility for each portfolio to the appropriate regional vice presidents. Then I give them the power to get the job done." Ted added that he reviews objectives periodically and keeps abreast of progress. "When my people feel they have problems beyond their realm, I will sit down with them and help them, although I generally discourage them from bringing me a problem without a recommended solution or two. I feel that to be a good manager, you have to spend a lot of time nurturing, encouraging, and at times, helping people get back on the right track; that's the key to getting the job done."

Sometimes, according to Ted, to really do a high quality job, you also have to take risks and not be afraid to press for projects you believe in. He said, "As in any large organization, you can be overwhelmed with the bureaucracy. Sometimes my staff will come to me with a recommendation to do something which is the right thing for the company and makes economic sense. Corporate management will say no because it might represent a new twist on things. Sometimes, I find I must take the risk, do some of these things and come back and demonstrate that they make sense. On the other hand, sometimes I feel I must keep on persisting and take it to a higher level to get it done."

One could also assume a "quality manager" has to have a sense of humor and have the finesse to turn around awkward or sensitive situations. At least in one case for Ted, an awkward situation turned into a gold mine.

"When I ran the mid-west region we negotiated the sale of a 50% interest in a major office/hotel complex with some Saudi national citizens. It was an intense negotiation process and we closed the deal in Paris, France, while sitting in a Rolls Royce parked in front of the Lido Theatre. Afterward we planned to have a follow-up meeting in Chicago. A few days later I was informed several Saudis, whom I had not met, would be arriving on a Sunday evening at Chicago's O'Hare airport. I called them, invited them out to dinner that night and told them I'd meet them at O'Hare. When I arrived at the airport I left my assistant and the limousine driver at the entrance and went in to meet the group. I missed them at the gate and proceeded to the baggage claim. There, upon seeing a middle eastern looking gentleman, I approached him, asked his name, identified myself and told him I was there to pick him up. He was visibly annoyed and distracted. In a huff he asked me why I didn't hold up a sign with his name as the other hosts did. I told him I forgot.

"When we got the car, he looked at the driver, looked at me, did a double take, and said, 'Oh my God, you're Mr. _____, I'm so sorry!' Well for the rest of the week, I could do no wrong. Now, that gentleman and I are very good friends. The key is that I didn't take it as an offense. I saw the humor and the opportunity to develop a good business relationship."

Angle View 5
STUNT PILOT AND THE SALT MINES
Julie - Stunt Show Pilot

To see Julie perform you have to look up. Way up! And while you're looking, prepare to be stunned and amazed as she defies gravity with grace and power. Julie is a professional air show performer and commercial airline pilot. In addition to her many stunt show performances throughout the United States, she was featured in a TV special on stunt pilots. Julie took Robin Leach on a special flight in which he remarked, "That wasn't like a roller coaster, it was more like the spin cycle of a washing machine."

What to Robin was a "spin cycle" is to Julie a very detailed, planned set of maneuvers that require top notch physical conditioning, split second timing, and supreme attention to detail. "My performance is actually choreographed to music. Each maneuver is planned so the audience can appreciate my moves while listening to music being played over the show's loudspeakers. One reason I do this is because my plane is much bigger than most planes used for stunts. I need much more sky for each maneuver. As an example, to do one loop requires over 1000 feet."

To achieve her high quality performance for which she is so well known, Julie has made her act a "cut above" by adding several extra touches. "I make my act more unusual and more desirable," she said, "by adding multi-colored smoke emissions and ground explosions along with the music. This makes my performance a more complete experience."

"I give myself high quality marks for a performance when I know I was able to overcome the exterior conditions, for example, high winds, low visibility, low ceiling or heavy rain, and still fly great. I can easily tell when I've flown 'great' versus just OK. Also, I can always tell by the crowds' reactions. They definitely affect my performance."

In her profession, quality is also directly affected by her physical conditioning. At times she is pulling up to six times her body weight due to the G forces on the airplane. To stay in shape, Julie does one hour of aerobics training every day. "I do it because it makes me feel better, but also because my career depends on my health. In addition, stunts take a lot out of you. It's very trying on

33

your body. They say doing fifteen minutes of hard aerobatics is like working an eight-hour day in the salt mines."

That extra stamina and strength are also needed to be ready for things that may go wrong. "One time my seat slid all the way back on its track during a maneuver. It took a lot of strength and focus but fortunately, I was able to get the plane right side up. For a few minutes it was a very dangerous situation."

Julie's on the go continuously. Dealing with the demands of a successful commercial piloting career and being a star stunt show performer seem to energize her. When asked how she does it all, she stressed the importance of being balanced and organized.

"I make time to do the things I want to do. I'll work real hard because I want some slack time, or I want to do my aerobics, or I want to take my dog for a nice walk. I am definitely not all work and no play. I plan my time well. This may be one part of being a perfectionist. What takes most people a whole day to do, I can do in half. When I make time for a project, I don't wait for tomorrow—I do it!"

"For example, last night I got home from a four-day trip. I have a day and a half off and then another trip. Last night the first thing I did was unpack my bag, do my laundry, refill my toilet kit, and get everything ready for the next trip. If I had to go right now, my bags are ready. I don't wait until the last minute on anything. It very well may be part of my training as an airline pilot. You have to be very organized to be a good pilot. You're doing so many tasks simultaneously that if you are not organized it could literally kill you."

The Angle on Chapter 3

Wow,
a new "angle"
on leadership and taking
risks! Michelle Carroll takes us
through a method of team leadership that
includes communication, exploring our comfort
zones, and creating an environment for others
to succeed. This chapter introduces a brand
new risk taking concept. Find out
what it means to go out on
a L-I-M-B.
RG

3

REAL LEADERSHIP &
RISK TAKING
Michelle A. Carroll

In this chapter we will explore some basic ideas about quality
leadership and what it takes to be an effective team leader. Some of
the areas we will cover are:

>   • Remembering the Basics of Communication
>   • Exploring our Comfort Zone - Stepping out on a L-I-M-B
>   • Creating an Environment for Others to Succeed

We will explore each of these areas in more detail and share stories
of how effective leaders handle their challenging situations. First
let's look at remembering the basics of communication.

REMEMBER THE BASICS?

Effective communication begins with a solid foundation. Whether you are sharing or gathering information from others, what you say as well as how you say it will determine the effectiveness of the interaction. It's critical to establish an understanding of how you will communicate. For example, if you are responsible for leading a staff, establishing agreement on the methods of communication within the group will increase your team's effectiveness. Lack of communication is a shared concern for both managers and employees, team leaders and team members. Conducting regular staff meetings, sharing pertinent information one-on-one, using bulletin boards and creating a routing folder to share information, are just a few examples of types of communication that might be appropriate for your situation. Conducting regular staff meetings sounds like a simple idea, doesn't it? Well, I remember a situation where a team of employees held regular staff meetings, however they were not very effective. No one in the group really understood what the others were doing which led to confusion and frustration. They were much more effective once they shared information about their individual responsibilities and understood how and where they all fit in support of a common vision.

To determine the best method of communication for situations you encounter, review the alternatives then explore which ones work best for you. The key is to determine the purpose and the expected outcome of the communication then decide upon the most effective method to use.

Let's explore the following basic ideas a leader should consider when communicating with others:

- Doing what you say you're going to do.
- Remembering to always listen to the other side of the story.
- Treating other people as you want to be treated.
- Doing the right thing by being "straight" with people.
- Listening to your "gut," then backing it up with facts.

First let's take a look at the impact leaders can make when they follow through on what they say they are going to do.

36

DO WHAT YOU SAY YOU'RE GOING TO DO

It's important to make a commitment and then keep it. One of the quickest ways to lose credibility is by not following through with what you say you're going to do. For example, a common situation that is easy to forget to follow through on is notifying candidates about the outcome of their interviews. Managers typically interview several candidates for one position. At the end of the interview the manager usually informs the candidate about the next step in the process. This is the critical point when leaders have the opportunity to follow through with what they said they were going to do. A lot of times it's easier to extend the offer to the selected candidate and forget to notify the others. It's more pleasant delivering the good news to the selected candidates than to inform the others the not so good news, for them. At this point, you could lose credibility by not following through with your commitments.

ZIP IT AND LISTEN TO THE OTHER SIDE

When you're discussing a situation it's important to ask the other person what he/she thinks and feels. Most of us are not mind readers and can make a much better decision after we hear what the other person has to say. It's critical to remember not to make a judgment until the other individual has an opportunity to explain his/her understanding of a situation.

Sometimes we tend to jump to conclusions without input from the other person thereby missing critical facts. Several years ago I worked with a manager who was concerned about conducting a performance review with one of her employees. The main reason for concern was that she really didn't know how the employee was going to react. After much discussion the manager realized she had never asked the employee how she felt things were going. They had conversations about the day to day activities within the department, however, they never really discussed how the employee would be evaluated. So before finalizing the evaluation, the manager had a conversation with the employee to gain an understanding of how she thought she was doing. To the manager's surprise the employee had been involved in a lot more than she realized. The manager took the employee's information into consideration when writing the evaluation. As it turned out the employee was very satisfied with the final evaluation. The manager learned how vital it is to listen to what the other person had to say.

THE GOLDEN RULE!

It's important to let the people you interact with know you care about them. I've had several conversations with managers wanting to fire one of their employees. The reasons varied from poor attendance to not meeting the managers' expectations (typically, the employees weren't really sure what their manager expected). In the case of poor attendance, the manager was upset because the employee was continuously late for work. Instead of discussing the unacceptable attendance with the employee, the manager just thought it would be easier to just let him go and hire someone else. After discussing the specifics of the situation with the employee, the manager realized he had not asked the employee for his perception of the situation. Open communication is critical when making tough decisions like this.

Also, the manager realized he would not want his manager to make such a rushed decision about the fate of his employment without considering all the facts. As it turned out the employee had personal reasons for being late and felt it was acceptable since his manager hadn't mentioned anything to him. When the manager understood why the employee was late he agreed to consider a different work schedule. The manager and the employee both felt they needed to be open and communicate more effectively with each other. From this experience the manager learned to put himself in the other person's shoes and have a little more compassion.

BE "STRAIGHT" UP WITH PEOPLE

A common tendency for some people is to avoid confrontations. It's better to clear the air and allow both parties to discuss the issue rather than have it bottle up inside and only get worse. The frustration may come out in other ways like snapping at a family member or friend. Be sensitive to the message you are delivering and how the receiver is going to hear it.

One situation that comes to mind is when an employee had a body odor problem and the manager couldn't bring himself to talk with the employee. The manager spent a lot of time worrying about what to do and hoping the problem would just go away. The problem did not go away and after many sleepless nights the manager decided to do the right thing and talk with the employee. The manager realized this was a delicate topic and he would need to be sensitive to the employees reaction. The employee did not realize he had a body odor problem and even though he was embarrassed by the situation he appreciated the feedback. Like any other employee concern, this should be handled in a timely and effective manner.

LISTEN TO YOUR GUT

A key responsibility of a leader is to ensure the right people are in the right jobs. Typically managers are faced with the challenge of staffing their departments. This may mean an additional person being added to their staff or a backfill for someone who has moved out of the group. What I am suggesting by listen to your "gut," then back it up with facts, is that we sometimes have a feeling about something but can't quite articulate what it is. I remember a situation when a manager was in a rush to fill an opening within his department. He interviewed a candidate who was not quite right, however, at first he could not figure out why. As it turned out the manager spoke with the candidate again and realized the candidate did not have the depth of knowledge the position required. Hiring the wrong person can be a very costly decision. It's important to take the time up front and validate your "gut" reaction. It's usually right! Ultimately being thorough will save both time and money.

Remember that basic communication skills like effective listening are the foundation for good leadership. In addition to enhancing communication skills, effective leaders allow themselves the opportunity to become aware of their comfort zones.

EXPLORING OUR COMFORT ZONE

Effective leaders must be willing to get to know themselves in order to be comfortable with who they really are and with what they're all about. We must all take responsibility for our actions and be honest with ourselves. Effective leaders understand they must be willing to change the things they can control. Part of understanding our comfort zone involves knowing our level of tolerance for risk taking. Some people choose to risk very little, while others seem to naturally crave it. Let's take a look at an old exercise along with a new idea about changing your mindset and doing some risk taking.

CHANGE YOUR MINDSET & TAKE RISKS

Try out a new idea. Instead of doing things the way you've always done them, stop, take a step back and ask yourself if there might be another way. By another way I mean a different way, not just doing the same thing more or better, I'm mean a totally different approach. Challenge yourself to try new things. I call this getting off the hamster wheel. Picture a hamster wheel going around and around and around not getting anywhere. The hamster can do more of the same thing by going faster and faster, but by jumping off the hamster wheel it becomes obvious that there's another way of life out there. Instead of spinning our wheels going round and round trying to do more or get better we sometimes have to stop and ask if there might be another way. So, try stopping the wheel, jump off and focus on what's important to you.

Let's take a moment to be creative and look at the nine dot exercise on the next page. You'll need a blank sheet of paper.

Note: Some of you may have already tried it. If so, think back to your first attempt to complete the exercise. How did you try to figure it out? Were you successful on your first attempt?—Your second? Did you have to see the answer?.

Please turn the page and follow the instructions.

DRAW THESE 9 DOTS
on a blank sheet of paper.

- • - • - •

- • - • - •

- • - • - •

Connect the nine dots with four straight lines. Without picking up your pencil, go through each dot only once.

(The solution is on page 49.)

THIS CAN GET SCARY

Let's take this nine dot example one step further. After seeing the solution did you realize it requires us to think differently and go outside the boundaries? What makes a person break out of the nine dots? The area drawn outside the nine dots is what I call stepping out on a L-I-M-B. By stepping out on a L-I-M-B we allow ourselves the opportunity to see and try different things.

Take a look at the diagram on the next page to get an idea of what stepping out on a L-I-M-B looks like.

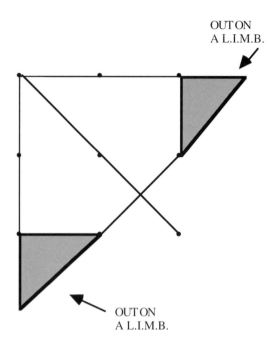

OUT ON
A L.I.M.B.

OUT ON
A L.I.M.B.

Going outside the nine dots allows us to see and try new things and take risks. Here are some details on the L-I-M-B concept.

RISK TAKING WITH L-I-M-B:

L	=	**Learning**
I	=	**Involvement**
M	=	**Mindset**
B	=	**Balance**

<u>Learning</u> - Challenge yourself to learn new skills. Focus on the excitement of learning something new and interesting. Continuous learning is a necessary process to develop skills that are valuable in the marketplace. Learning can occur through a formal program or self development on your own by reading, researching, and requesting information interviews.

<u>Involvement</u> - Develop and maintain a network of individuals that will encourage, challenge, and support you. Have the courage to engage in a variety of new activities. Tap into your network of friends, colleagues, and other business associates. Tap into

organizations, both professional and personal, that are of interest to you.

Mindset - Keep an open mind about new ideas and be willing to leave your comfort zone. Look at things differently—not only better and faster; try a new approach.

Balance - Become aware and focus on your priorities and values to really enjoy your life. Maintain your health and well-being.

PERSONALLY...JUST HANGING ON!

After experiencing many changes and feeling like I was stuck on the hamster wheel I decided it was time to break out of my nine dot thinking. I stepped out on a L-I-M-B by:

Learning - Becoming aware of my current skill set. I began by creating a personal development plan that focused on learning new skills.

Involvement - I got involved with several people who were inspiring, encouraging, and supportive of my plans and ideas.

Mindset - I opened my mind to see and do things differently. I made a conscious effort to learn to take risks and leave my comfort zone.

Balance - Here is where I determined the values that are important in my life and how each one complements the others.

TRY CLIMBING THIS TREE!

When I think of this L-I-M-B concept, I visualize a sturdy redwood tree with solid roots as the foundation for continuous learning and growth. As we challenge ourselves to learn, our roots become more solid. The tree trunk represents involvement whereby developing a nurturing support network helps us grow. The many branches encourage us to change our mindset and seek out different paths. Finally, it's critical to keep balance by not going too far to either extreme causing the tree to grow unevenly.

Another way to describe stepping out on a L-I-M-B is with the following model:

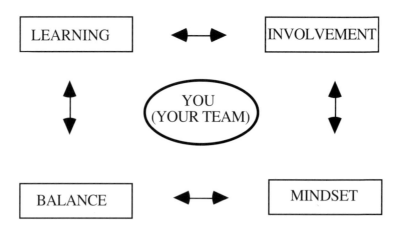

The arrows represent the importance of focusing on all four areas at the same time.

Stepping outside the boundaries can be the beginning of a challenging and exciting time. To develop your own personal action plan for stepping out on a L-I-M-B see the worksheet inventory at the end of the chapter.

In addition to remembering the basics of communication and exploring comfort zones, another key area leaders consider is creating an environment for others to succeed.

HELP OTHERS TO SUCCEED

Effective leaders understand they have the ability to create a positive environment which encourages others to succeed. This includes setting the stage for an employee to reach his/her full potential. As a leader, you can play a vital support role when employees choose to become aware of their boundaries and step out on a L-I-M-B. Creating a stimulating work setting will encourage people to learn and grow.

A term I often hear is "Walk the Talk." What this means is that people should say the right things as well as display consistent actions. Working in an environment where leaders consistently act upon what they say sets a good example for others to follow. When leading by example leaders demonstrate the behaviors so others know what to expect. One of the most consistent comments I've heard from employees over the years is that management doesn't care. "They" (whoever they are) don't set a good example. There seems to be one set of rules for management and another set for employees. So when creating the optimum environment for others to succeed, keep in mind actions speak louder than words.

When setting the stage for others to succeed it's beneficial to involve others in decision making and encourage their personal commitment. The key is to learn what motivates each individual within the group and then create the support mechanism for him/her to succeed. Open, honest communication is necessary for both personal and professional growth. Effective leaders allow others to learn from their own mistakes. It's important for all of us to accept responsibility for developing ourselves. After all, we are the best judge of determining our interests and willingness to learn new skills. However, an effective leader plays a critical role of coach, advisor, and supporter. A common trap we sometimes fall into is expecting someone else, usually our immediate manager, to take responsibility for our development. It's critical that the manager and employee mutually agree on the employee's development plan.

So, remember to ask your staff or team what you can do to help them develop themselves. Listen and learn from your staff on an ongoing basis. Ask your staff for feedback on how well you're doing to support them. This approach will help you determine where you are in terms of coaching your staff and if you should make any changes in your own development plan. You might gain some insight that otherwise would not have been shared. I've worked for a few leaders who asked what else they could do to support me. I really appreciated the opportunity to let them know what I needed from them to accomplish my goals.

I can't emphasize enough that we are all responsible for our own development but knowing you have a caring support system makes a world of difference. When creating the climate, consider using recognition and feedback as a means to let people know that they are valued, respected, and supported.

RECOGNITION

Effective leaders know it's important to recognize others for their contribution. This includes people directly on your staff as well as others. When thinking of recognition in general, I remember a time when I was impressed with one of the speakers at a management status meeting. The reason he stood out is that he didn't take all the credit for the success of a project. He actually acknowledged other people who didn't report directly to him. He mentioned it so naturally you could tell he was truly appreciative. There's a big difference between being sincere, and just going through the motions.

The opportunity to recognize others can occur in many different situations and be accomplished in a variety of ways. I've worked with several managers who realize the value of recognizing others. Some of the things they did to reward others was to take the person or team to lunch, present cash awards and write thank you letters. So, ask yourself if you are spending enough time looking at things people do right. A simple "thank you" goes a long way. Remember to be timely, specific and tell people why you are recognizing them. In addition to recognizing others, it's also important for leaders to provide feedback.

FEEDBACK...BACK...BACK!

Giving constructive feedback is an opportunity to let people know where they stand and where they are heading in terms of their performance. Employees deserve honest feedback on a regular basis. Feedback can be given in a positive situation to acknowledge and support current performance. It can also be delivered for corrective purposes to guide the employee back on track toward acceptable performance. Let's take a closer look at positive and corrective feedback:

As you will see, effective feedback, whether it's the positive or the corrective type, should genuinely value the individual. It also helps if the feedback is:
- timely
- specific
- usually private (corrective)
- honest

POSITIVE FEEDBACK

Delivering positive feedback can be a very rewarding event. It usually makes the person receiving the feedback feel valued. For example, if an employee completes work assignments on time or early and their manager acknowledges that behavior it reminds the employee they are on the right track with their performance. Researchers have shown it over and over. The best way to get good results without negative side effects, is with positive feedback. It requires skill and timing on the part of the manager or leader.

CORRECTIVE FEEDBACK

One of the most difficult tasks for a leader is to deliver corrective feedback. Sometimes we think it is easier to ignore the situation and it will go away. Usually it only gets worse. For example, if an employee is having a difficult time completing work assignments and the issue is not addressed, the manager could find that some critical deadlines were not met because they didn't discuss the situation. Creating an environment where others are valued will encourage open communication between both parties and make difficult situations more manageable.

WIIFM - "WHAT'S IN IT FOR ME?"

When thinking about applying some of the ideas mentioned in this chapter you may ask yourself WIIFM - "What's In It For Me?"
What's in it for you is a better understanding of yourself so you can be more effective in interactions with others. When you are involved in a situation it's also important to consider the WIIFM from the other person's eyes.

When remembering the basics of communication, the WIIFM for the manager and the employee (or team leader and team members) is more effective two way communication. The manager will become a more effective and compassionate communicator and the employee will feel supported and respected.

When exploring comfort zones the WIIFM for both the manager and the employee is the opportunity to better understand their current level of comfort with risk taking and their ability to step outside the boundaries.

When creating an environment for others to succeed, the WIIFM for the manager is happier, fulfilled, productive employees, which ultimately affects the bottom line. The WIIFM for employees is to be supported and encouraged to fulfill their goals.

IN SUMMARY

Effective leaders understand the importance of remembering to communicate effectively, exploring their comfort zones, and creating environments for others to succeed.

Remember the basics of communication. Do what you say you're going to do; listen to the other side of the story; treat other people as you want to be treated; do the right thing by being "straight" with people; listen to your "gut," then back it up with facts.

When taking risks, know your boundaries and determine when it's appropriate to go outside the nine dots. Consider stepping out on a L-I-M-B by continuously *learning*, being *involved* with others, shifting your *mindset* and keeping a perspective on *balance*.

Realize the value of recognition and feedback when creating an environment for others to succeed. More importantly, keep in mind the WIIFM for those you interact with, as well as for yourself.

SOLUTION TO DOT EXERCISE:

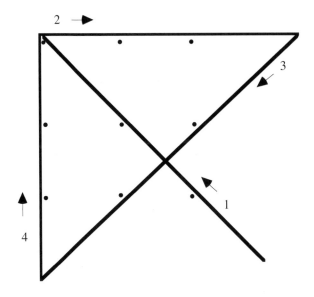

POINTS TO REMEMBER/THINGS TO DO

1. Follow through on commitments.
2. Listen to the other side of the story.
3. Treat others as you would want to be treated, always being "straight up" with people.
4. Avoid the "Tantalus" Complex by being open and truthful.
5. Listen to your "gut" for the best decision or action to take.
6. Explore your comfort zones—step out on a L-I-M-B.
7. Create an environment for others to succeed.
8. Remember the WIIFM (what's in it for me?).

L-I-M-B RISK TAKING INVENTORY

Use this sheet to outline ways to grow and expand. Set some dates for when you will reach milestones in each of the areas below.

GOAL #1
LEARNING: Target Date:
Activities to Pursue: _____

_____

_____

_____

GOAL #2
INVOLVEMENT: Target Date:

Activities to Pursue: _____

_____

_____

_____

GOAL #3
MINDSET: Target Date:

Activities to Pursue: _____

_____

_____

_____

GOAL #4
BALANCE: Target Date:

Activities to Pursue: _____

_____

_____

_____

(Permission granted to copy this form after purchase of book)

Angle View 6
FROM A HOUSE TO A HOME
Verne - Executive Director, Foster Home Licensing Agency

Verne is the executive director of a non-profit corporation that licenses, trains, and supervises foster homes in eight California counties. One of the main components of his job is to talk with members of the religious community, primarily churches, to recruit people interested in becoming foster parents to the many young boys and girls unable to co-exist peacefully with their own families. Additionally, he is responsible for the hiring and management of his staff and the training and supervision of the approximately 30 homes he has recruited to date. The homes are subject to certain regulations and Verne must make sure they are run in adherence with his own standards as well as the requirements of the county and state agencies.

Working with a variety of agencies and personalities often is the source of a great deal of frustration for Verne. Certainly the dynamics of his reporting arrangements are more complex than a standard line of command. This can create conflicts with Verne's desire to smoothly run a quality operation.

"This county is very bureaucratic. The employees tend to be so power conscious; they want to control. They want to march into our homes and superimpose themselves. It creates a real chaos in terms of communication. Our homes operate under our management and yet they have to take instruction from the county agencies. I address the conflict with the county very forthrightly. I find myself bucking heads over who is going to manage our homes, the county or us. It hasn't resulted in any children being removed from our custody, but in all honesty, to protect the integrity of the homes, I would have to do that."

"In fact, if I get through a week and did not have to deal with a serious difference with the county or anyone, I feel I've done a good, high quality job. There are an awful lot of opportunities for things to slip through the cracks and for differences of opinion in this business. You have to understand the dynamics of what we work with: disturbed kids, quality homes, and agencies that are overworked. If we can meet everyone's needs with a minimum of arguing and quarreling, I've had a successful week."

51

Verne also feels successful when he sees the people that he hires and those running the foster homes handling their own areas of responsibility in a capable manner. He said he does not feel he is performing at his highest level if he needs to constantly look over their shoulders, reviewing and overseeing every detail. "I only want to be involved when it looks like I need to lend a hand or direction or some kind of counsel because of my background or considerable experience as a foster parent. Otherwise I tend to let those with whom I manage wrestle with the issues and in the long run I think that helps them become stronger individuals. I'm not a real hands-on manager."

Turnover for foster homes can be very high. In some cases, a county can lose as many homes as it recruits in a year. Verne attributes this to improper training, preparation and support on the part of most agencies. His operation has a very low turnover rate. Verne explains, "I lay out a very specific picture of the demands of the job. Our orientation is very specific, very honest and very frank. We tell them up front how difficult foster care is. I'd rather they eliminate themselves in the beginning."

Verne's advice for insuring a high quality performance is to find in your heart what you want to do and start stepping in that direction. "You'll do well," he says, "if your job can give you the inner satisfaction of accomplishing something and being fulfilled." He and his wife have been running a foster home for 20 years. After years of also working as a banking executive, Verne made a bold step to stop what he didn't enjoy and get more involved with the foster care system. He's happy now, although he admits his life is not quite in balance.

"Some people, even my wife, might say we are out of balance, but her desire is so much like mine; we are running in the same direction, same career track, same motivation, and the same goals. That's unique, you're not going to find many couples that have experienced that."

Angle View 7
"GIVE ME YOUR MONEY"
Victoria - Professional Fund-raiser

"For my job as a professional fund-raiser, the most important attributes for success are being a self starter and having good self esteem," said Victoria. She went on, "You have to love yourself and know that you can do anything in the world you want to if you put your mind to it. I know I can do anything I want if I try."

Victoria put her philosophy to work just to get her a job. She did not have the standard qualifications for the position which included a college degree and five to six years of sales experience, but she felt strongly that she could do it, and do it successfully. "I had a friend who ranted and raved about her job as a fund-raiser. I had never heard anyone be that excited about her job before so I asked her to tell me why it was so great and how I might get involved. I didn't have any of the required experience, nor a college degree, but I was motivated. I wanted that job and went after it. In fact it was because I was so persistent that the company granted me an interview."

Victoria's responsibility is to visit schools to find teachers, classes, athletic programs or clubs that need to raise money. Her company has an extensive product line of items such as wrapping paper, candy and chocolates available for sale. The students choose the items they want to sell. Victoria puts on a motivational kick-off presentation to get the group excited, and then they "hit the streets." Perhaps some of her enthusiasm rubs off on her students, said Victoria. "I encourage them to go after their goal and not concentrate on the prizes for top selling. I rather make it a group effort toward the objective they have in mind. It's all about having a positive attitude."

Victoria is energetic, positive, and committed to the highest standards of quality in her job. "I always stay away from negative people and negative situations. I listen to positive thinking tapes when I'm driving and when I'm sleeping. It's easy to say 'just think positive.' It's harder to do it. I listen to the same tapes over and over and over. Eventually I find you can replace old beliefs that are negative with new positive beliefs. You can actually change your frame of mind and way of thinking."

53

Another key attribute for Victoria is approach. Her peers in the business, she says, tend to be older and have a different selling philosophy. She feels they are a bit too forward and aggressive in seeking contracts. "I'm there for the kids. I have my own four-year old and I love kids. I also appreciate what the teachers are doing and I tell them. I know that without their special efforts, especially in times budget cuts, downsizing and layoffs, the children would suffer. Teachers are overworked and underpaid. This is especially true for the teachers who take on special programs or extracurricular activities, often without extra compensation."

Because attitude and approach are so important to success for Victoria, she also emphasizes the need for her life to be in order. "For me there are three bodies. To be in balance I must be as much into the spiritual side of me, as I am into the physical, as I am into the emotional. This is the hardest thing in the world. Since we all live in the physical, we have to make a concerted effort to promote the spiritual and the emotional. The spiritual side is not really promoted in this day and age as much as it should be. For the emotional, I try to spend quiet time with myself and I spend time with my son. When my physical, emotional and spiritual sides are in balance, things are more peaceful; things seem to flow easier. I can ask myself a question and get an answer. Rather than searching 'out there,' I can go within. Balance for me is relaxing; it lets me know I'm not just living for a paycheck."

Certainly "living for a paycheck" is not the primary goal of this quality-oriented woman. For Victoria, feeling great is paramount. To feel great, she suggests people make a list of everything they do well. She stresses some may feel this is a difficult task at first, but if they really look within, they would be surprised at how much they do well. She said, "read your list and feel good about yourself. Allow yourself to say "I'm great; I can be me better than anyone else in his whole wide world."

The Angle on Chapter 4

*What
is an acid test?
Is it really a fool-proof
way of spotting the genuine
article? This chapter will give
you the test that you can apply in a bank line
or at the grocery check out counter to see if
the service meets the standard. Speaking
of standards, here is where you'll also
read about the three performance
standards - Perfection,
Average, and
Stretch.
RG*

4

SETTING & MEASURING STANDARDS
Rick Griggs

Remember the advice Napoleon got from Louis Marquis de Fontanes about always being perfect..."the desire of perfection is the worst disease that ever afflicted the human mind." This may be an exaggeration but it does open the door to the possibility that perfection should not <u>always</u> be the goal. Being appropriate is more reasonable and still meets the criteria for quality.

This chapter will present the case that in setting and measuring standards in your department you should not be tempted to haul out the old slogans from previous motivational sessions where you shot for the moon. No one can argue with "reach for the top," "good enough isn't," "quality is job one," and all the others. Well, good enough is if that's what the customer wants and needs. This allows for the prioritization of when the customer calls and asks for perfection, when they just want to pay for average, and which cases need the extra push to match exactly what the customer wants and expects to pay for.

An example of the wrong standards being applied was when I took my Jeep in for service. It was mid-winter and they called me at home to say they had a special on re-charging the air conditioning system. I thought "who needs that now?" With the special promotion I decided to go ahead and do it. They did a wonderful job on my air conditioning unit but left the cap off of my power steering fluid reservoir. I would have preferred less time "perfecting" my air conditioning system and more attention paid to something I'd need on every turn in the road.

Here's a new twist on looking at standards. There is a place for perfection but it's not in all areas. The place for it is where it's needed. There are also appropriate applications for average performance and stretch performance. Of course, all of this is based on what the customer wants and needs.

- Option 1: <u>PERFECTION</u> (no mistakes, zero defects)
- Option 2: <u>AVERAGE</u> (past results are fine)
- Option 3: <u>STRETCH</u> (reasonable difficulty)

DON'T BUILD THE HABIT OF FAILING

Set the right standard from the beginning. Average is very acceptable for some well-defined situations. Others require stretch or perfection standard options. Quality is picking the right one at the beginning and then getting agreement on it as the correct standard. If you've ever heard anyone say "enough is enough," "let's just move on," or "it's already fine...let's press ahead," you've heard someone who is frustrated over the wrong standard selection. Some shoppers want the best tomatoes, but the cheapest paper towels. Some car owners want perfect brake jobs but low octane gasoline. People pick where they want the best and where they want to save time and money by accepting lower level products or services. This is the moment of truth in selecting appropriate standards for performance at work and in personal life. We build the failure habit by saying we never let down, always do perfect work, and our relationships are always top-notch. We do let down, no one can possibly be perfect, and the only perfect relationships are perhaps on the evening TV shows or at the cinema.

THE "ACID TEST" FOR QUALITY

Just how do you light a match that illuminates quality? Is there really a quick and useful way to compare what you do and what others do to some valuable standard? We think there is, and believe it or not, it doesn't have to be complicated or detailed. It may not be as easy as tapping your heels together and saying "there's no place like home," but you can do something quickly, that spells the word Q-U-A-L-I-T-Y. The acid test for quality is Q-MATCh. It's easy to say, it's easy to remember, but not always a breeze to practice.

QUALITY = "Q-MATCh"

You can apply this acid test to yourself and the important things you do or to others and the critical items they have agreed to perform. The terms and changes are not always plastered across an ad in the daily paper. In such an ad most terms and changes would be fairly clear. In many cases the terms and changes are simply <u>implied</u>. It might not seem just, but quality is judged on implications as much as on written contracts—we can say that Quality...
- Meets
- Agreed
- Terms &
- Changes

When you're in these situations ask yourself if the service or activity really does <u>Meet</u> <u>Agreed</u> <u>Terms</u> and <u>Changes</u>?

- At your favorite restaurant?
- At the cleaners?
- Getting your car washed?
- Service at a hospital?
- Getting magazines delivered?
- Repaying an IOU?
- Borrowing computer equipment from a business friend?
- Showing up for group rehearsal?

If it Meets Agreed Terms & Changes—it's Quality! Remember, although there are different levels of performance, the test is whether it matches what was agreed. Quality at the personal level can mean getting the boy or girl to deliver the paper anywhere on the lawn or specifically to the door mat. Both are quality if they are agreed on. You can also change the requirement by asking that they put the paper behind the fence so it won't get wet or stolen. This new change now defines the performance needed—in other words the level of quality.

You may have noticed that some of these personal quality standards make you feel uncomfortable. By quickly reading them you have already compared them to your own personal expectations and you've made a judgment call as to their being too strict or too lenient.

A CLOSE LOOK AT "Q-MATCh"

Now, we get to something that makes life tough for many people. Quality is not perfection or goodness. Quality at work or at home is meeting expectations. We can select the expectation that best fits the need. Sometimes it means zero mistakes or defects, while at other times less-than-perfect performance still gives us what we require. It still must Meet Agreed Terms and Changes.

PERFECTION...IS IT POSSIBLE?

The perfection option is for those times when it's okay to put other things on the back burner to allow this top priority to get full attention, financial support, and all available resources. It's obvious that this standard blows many other priorities out of the water and therefore should be chosen correctly and appropriately. "Top of the line" examples of the perfection standard include:
- correspondence - customer letters, proposals, and requests
- eating/hotels - four, five star restaurants and hotels
- house cleaning - deep cleaning for parties, dinners, entertaining

We find a poor example in the emission controls policy for automobiles in states with heavy smog problems. California, for instance, instituted a perfection standard of requiring all autos purchased after a certain year to be tested for smog emissions every

two years. They found that the automobiles required to get smog
checks (88%) were responsible for no more than 20% of the smog
emissions. It was the 12% of exempt autos that were producing
most of the problem. The time, energy and financial resources were
arguably "perfected" at the wrong problem.

AVERAGE STANDARD

The average option is the lowest of the three quality standards. Low
does not mean bad or unacceptable. This standard option recognizes
that past performance has been just fine. Everyone is pleased and
would rather you put your time and effort into priorities needing
higher levels of performance. "Leaving well enough alone" might
be the catch phrase for the average standard. Most of what we do
must fall into this area. Here are some examples in this category:
  • correspondence - internal only memos, hand written
  instructions, rough drafts
  • eating/hotels - cafe or deli lunch counter service, overnight
  motel stay for early meeting
  • house cleaning - mid-week straightening up for a pot luck

S-T-R-E-T-C-H STANDARD

The stretch option requires better performance than the average
option. This one takes you to higher octane, better communication,
and additional compliance. It does not soak up all your time and
effort by turning into a quest for perfection when all that is
appropriately needed is better performance. Here are the examples
for this type of standard:
  •correspondence - inter-office memos and correspondence,
  letters to colleagues, friends
  •eating/hotels - casual dinner meeting, annual vacations
  •house cleaning - weekly, monthly regular cleaning

An office example is having the secretary type notes from a training
class into the computer. These notes will be corrected and re-
arranged at a later date but the activity helps the manager prioritize,
add, and delete information, while keeping the office clutter to a
minimum. The stretch standard is appropriate for doing the work
properly but not wasting time that can be applied to a client letter that
really needs perfection.

MEASURING PERSONAL STANDARDS?

Measuring personal goals and standards can get sticky. What's important is that your personal yardstick is used so you'll know if you're on the right track. Many people will measure according to subjective feelings (good or bad), reports from other (important) people or feelings of general happiness. Still others will chose not to measure anything. They feel a disdain for the dirty deed of measuring. They may have experienced an unfair situation where measurement was not performed properly or was used in a negative manner. It will take a lot to make them trust the system again. This is okay, as long as they realize that this means sacrificing a tool that helps. It's like digging a hole without a shovel. It's okay and it will get done, but perhaps not as efficiently as someone else who chooses to use the shovel.

Personal Quality Standards are measured a bit differently than your standards at work. Personal standards result from your values, attitudes, and opinions. This relates to your personal and family life. Any measurement ideas you might have will do, as long as they move you toward, rather than away from what you want. Sometimes they simply come from your intuitive judgment. Work standards are beginning to include more of the subjective measures but, by and large, work performance must be more quantifiable, observable, and results-oriented.

MEASURING QUALITY

What's important to you? The answer to this question will determine what, and how much you will need to measure. Kids count marbles, merchants count dollars, and Casanovas counts dates! Everything we do can be measured. Personal quality measurement may include subjective or "softer" versions of measurement. Sometimes this will involve things like feelings, relationships or other emotional kinds of issues.

Although softer forms of measurement are valid, in the work setting we need to be more exact and accountable. Here is where more observable and tangible forms of measurement are most useful. A good measurement system will pinpoint performance while leaving room for some of the "intuitive" measures as well.

THE BIG "MISSION" PICTURE

Measurement should not begin until the larger focus has been examined. For a business, it's the mission statement and success factors, for an agency it might be the charter and funding agency expectations. On the home front, this might include a family plan or value system combined with general agreements. The point being that every person should read from the same script. There are two ideal benefits to clearing up the big picture, first, everyone becomes clear on the concept. The "raison d'etre" or the glue that holds that particular group of people together becomes apparent. Second, you will see an immediate jump in cohesiveness, synergy, and directedness following a focused look at the mission, charter or value agreements. As our business began to grow during the 80's and early 90's there was no time to track and measure all the activities of all the people. It would have been a business disaster to even try. Instead, I became an obnoxious bore by repeatedly focusing on our mission, success factors, values, and department charters. This master plan or, as we called them, our "six golden pages," gave us the direction, priorities, and measurement parameters we needed and still allowed for individual performance and initiative.

The success factors are the 8-12 items that must be implemented to fully support the mission, charter or family value system. In a business, these 8-12 success factors can form the basis for various job descriptions and measurement results indicators. In other words, they are the essential items that result in the mission being accomplished. When there's confusion or uncertainty, the success factors often hold the key for prioritizing and setting standards.

NOW, GRAB THE TAPE MEASURE!

It's a good idea to collect information to see where you stand before trying to impact performance. This baseline data is used as a benchmark to see how effective future changes and efforts will be in improving performance. Lousy data leads to lousy decisions. Take the time to measure well and get those being measured to support the idea. It's okay to measure outside of the work area. What gets measured gets done. If it's going to the gym, dinner and talks with loved ones or money in the savings account, when you measure it you do more of it. It also goes the other way. If you're trying to eliminate something, the measurement can help you move it in that direction also. This applies to weight loss, losing one's temper, too much television or skipping family gatherings.

WHAT...TO MEASURE

The process of deciding what to measure is a fundamental decision in the quality improvement effort. This one monumental act sets the priority for all effort, discussion, reward, and punishment. First you have to have a reason for doing something before it's of any use to measure. The reason is the mission, the charter or the set of values a group decides upon. Wrong measures are often tossed around to cover up poor performance. "I've been working so many hours I just couldn't complete the assignment." This implies that hours at work are the key measurement when the assignment is actually more fundamental than the hours. "I spent the whole weekend with you, what more do you want?" Here we have physical presence being counted as the measure when the real issue may have been mutual understanding, problems solved or time touching each other. What to measure is the make or break point for most serious endeavors. The correct answer will lead to the correct players being involved. The right answer will identify who or what isn't working. Finally the right answer to what to measure, will rally the troops around the core cause that brought the group together.

- Quantity (marbles, dollars, dinners, pages)
- Cost (dollars, over budget, under budget, profit, loss, break-even)
- Time (minutes, hours, over time, under time, time saved)
- Accuracy (mistakes, defects, proximity, inches, preciseness, corrections)
- Flexibility (speed in changing, adapting to new requirements)
- Balance (well-roundedness, symmetry, general equilibrium)

WHEN...TO MEASURE

Take care not to offend good people trying to do good work. Some may interpret this as childish activity on your part and treating them like children on the other end. It's usually a matter of tact and involvement. Talk to them and get them involved with the question of when is the best time to measure without creating more problems.

The best time to measure is when you can get the most accurate picture of what's happening. This "snap-shot" should record reality without affecting the results. If the measurement affects the results you are not recording performance, but the reaction to the measurement. Sometimes you want to do this—use measurement as a motivator. Since you know that what gets measured gets done you can use this wisely to motivate around certain issues. The draw-back is that it no longer records reality but actually changes it.

TOOLS FOR MEASURING

Customer surveys and assessments can be time consuming but this data is most useful in making decisions and measuring progress.

Before and After measures (pre-test, post-test) can be tricky due to other circumstances that might account for change or no change. As a general measure, these can be good for quick insights into how much change has occurred.

Primary data that you collect yourself avoids some misinterpretation. Secondary data you get from others saves lots of time and energy. This can be expensive if purchased from a source that makes a living by selling information.

Line graphs are where the individual data points are charted over days/weeks/months and connected with a line. These are what you see most often along with the bar graphs.

Bar graphs are where cumulative data is stacked in bar form to show comparisons of total time, money, defects or hours worked. This side-by-side eyeballing is quick and easy. Watch out for the legends on the Y axis. This is the percentage, dollars or defects that each bar is measuring. Bars can look very different if the Y (vertical) axis only goes from 92% to 100% instead of 0% to 100%.

Control charts are line or bar graphs that are used along with horizontal lines to show the upper and/or lower limits of acceptable performance. It's like the side boundaries on a volley ball court, as long as you're in-between them, you're okay.

Control circles are a new addition to the Macro Balance assessment tool. Like the lines on control charts, the space between the two concentric circles signifies where the measurement is within specification.

REMEMBER, WHEN YOU MEASURE

Many managers and team leaders with the best intentions have had their measurement strategies blow up in their faces. A common reaction is just to back off and let them "do what they want." This is short term and can lead to some major problems. Try these ideas to make it work.

- Inform people about the measurement system.
- Give the reasons for measuring.
- Let people know what will happen with the results.
- Measure in a way that performance does not react to the act of measuring.
- Measure unobtrusively without "spying."

When the system runs well you reap major competitive advantages. By minimizing efforts <u>away</u> from your goals, you and your group can avoid the negative effects of that wasteful "Tantalus" Complex.

POINTS TO REMEMBER/THINGS TO DO

1. Don't assume slogans of perfection are what customers want to hear.
2. The best thing you can do for customers is to meet their wants and needs.
3. Exceed customer wants and needs, as long as this does not cause you to neglect other customer issues.
4. There's nothing better than a good and fair measurement system.
5. Measure in a way that captures efforts and results connected to prevention. This is more important than crisis reduction.
6. Whatever gets measured gets done. Don't build frustration by measuring areas out of people's control.
7. Avoid "Tantalus"—Don't move toward and away from goals at the same time.

Department Measurement Inventory

Team leaders and members can take this inventory for an overview
of the measurement system in place within the organization.

Scoring: 1 = lowest, disagree, 3 = average, 5 = highest, agree

1. Our department measures items related to prevention.
       1   2   3   4   5

2. Our measurement system is simple and clean.
       1   2   3   4   5

3. We study and analyze the ingredients of prevention.
       1   2   3   4   5

**4. Our end goals and results are clearly stated and
understood by all.**
       1   2   3   4   5

5. Our end goals match our values.
       1   2   3   4   5

6. We measure major items that directly affect results.
       1   2   3   4   5

**7. Our results indicators (5-7 measures of success) are
visibly posted.**
       1   2   3   4   5

8. Our results indicators are kept current and accurate.
       1   2   3   4   5

9. Our system leads to better products and services.
       1   2   3   4   5

**10. Our measurement system leads to satisfied internal
and external customers.**
       1   2   3   4   5

TOTAL MEASUREMENT SYSTEM SCORE _____

(Permission granted to copy this form after purchase of book)

Angle View 8
FLYING ACES, "NEWBIES" & SURVIVAL
Pat - Navy Blue Angel Pilot

The Blue Angels are perhaps the most famous flying demonstration squadron in the world. Their reputation for precision flying is unmatched. These talented pilots are known for flying in their trademark diamond formation where it seems their wings almost touch as they whiz by. They do it well and they do it a lot! Blue Angels put on shows every weekend for four million people, nine months out of each year.

Talk about standards of quality! Quality is the hallmark of the team. In this elite profession standards of quality have been prescribed for the synchronization of a maneuver, the closeness of a formation, and even the timing of a handshake. At any given time there are only six Blue Angel pilots in the world. And Pat is one of them!

Pat, a second year team member, is the airborne safety coordinator. This is no small responsibility! "I fly in the back center of the diamond. I move everybody around into the formation positions. From my position I can see all the wingmen and our position over the ground. I'm responsible for the wingmen not hitting each other."

Needless to say, this type of responsibility is not given to just anyone. The selection process is tough? Competition is high; requirements are challenging. And requirements go way beyond one's piloting skill. Pat remarked, "Being selected is based more on personality, suitability for the team, willingness to learn, and ability to take instruction and accept criticism. You also must not be too egotistical. Your talent as a pilot is necessary of course, but the other personal traits are paramount in determining how you will succeed as a member of the team.

Blue Angels fly F18 Navy fighters. These are the same as the ones currently used in the Navy fleet with just a couple of modifications. (And a fantastic paint job!) Each Blue Angel spends two years putting on shows demonstrating performance maneuvers, dangerous near misses, and spectacular team flying techniques.

What's a quality Blue Angel performance? "A good solid air show," said Pat. "It must have been safe and completely in line with the plan. Every minute of every air show is videotaped from the time we walk out to the airplanes. The tape doesn't stop until after we have greeted the crowd to shake hands at the end. Afterward, each performance is critiqued from the audience's perspective. Details such as when we were out of position, when the smoke didn't come out at the proper time or when a handshake was late, are brought up. Details are discussed that even the audience might not notice. These debriefings last up to 2 hours."

"The common joke," he continued, "is we try to fly a perfect air show but it can't be done." But they try. A mistake, even small, is critical. It's no joke that the ability to take criticism is one of the criteria for the assignment. If you make a mistake, be prepared to hear about it, relive it, and get advice on making the necessary correction for the next performance, Pilots will often spend additional hours reviewing the tapes looking for errors and planning appropriate strategies for improving on the next outing.

New team members, called "newbies," are indoctrinated quickly. "A newbie is a member who hasn't flown before a million people yet," Pat said jokingly. "After a performance, newbies aren't allowed to say very much. They have to be able to sit there and listen to me telling them what they've done wrong. They need to be able to understand what went wrong, admit it, and then make the necessary corrections to keep the performances up to par. All of us have to be able to say, I screwed that up, now how can I do better next time?"

How can it be done better next time? Pat's advice—Ask. "If I'm having trouble with a maneuver, I'll call on other guys who have done it in the past. You never really leave the team. The ties are strong. We tend to lean on each other. I can guarantee you that the next person who takes my job will call me at home at night to discuss various maneuvers."

What gets in the way of doing a quality performance? "Our emotions and our family and friends," he said. "We fly every day of the week. You must maintain good relationships with the team members. If you're mad at someone, you can be distracted. When you're flying, that kind of distraction is unacceptable. As for family distractions, when you have a lot of family and friends in town, they tend to want to go to the air show, meet the team members, maybe have you go out to dinner, etc. We live in a strict routine and often have to disappoint them."

Try this for a routine: Up at 4:30 am (one cup of coffee), to work by 5:15 am (second cup of coffee), briefing from 6:15 to 7:00 am, 7:15 walk to jets, take a 1 1/2 hour flight until 9:00 am, debrief until 10: 45 am, have a 50 minute lunch, take second 1 1/2 hour flight, debrief again, and end the work day by spending 2 hours in the gym to relieve stress and get exercise. Whew!

As you might expect, this hectic lifestyle plays havoc with one's attempt to strike a balance between work, home, family, and other pursuits. Fortunately it's not a career long lifestyle. It's only a two-year stint. Pat credits his wife with giving him the support and encouragement to do his best during this temporary assignment. "My wife's my best fan and supports me 100%. She deserves a medal of honor for doing it."

To perform well, Pat offered three key components. "You must have personal integrity, you must be able to honestly accept your faults, and you must enjoy your job." Pat obviously seems to follow his own advice.

Angle View 9
YOUNG GUNS—BRIGHT EYES
Kamna - Student Leader, University

Kamna is a college junior at a California university majoring in rhetoric and communication. In addition to her studies, she is in her second year as a resident advisor to the 70 people in her dormitory. Technically, she said, it is supposed to be a 19 1/2 hour a week job, but it actually requires a full time commitment. For room and board, Kamna serves as a student advisor, counselor and policy enforcer.

For someone almost 19 years old, Kamna has a remarkably mature outlook on achieving and maintaining high standards on the job. The same skills she values as an on-campus leader apply to anyone already in a leadership role or aspiring to that goal.

"One thing that makes quality work is dedication from the person and commitment to the job. To do a quality job you have to put time and effort into it. You can't just go through the moves. Also people need to believe in what they are doing. For example, I probably wouldn't do quality work if I were a painter because I don't like painting. You have to enjoy your job to put out quality work. In the simplest sense, I know when something is of high quality when I can look at my outcome and say yes, I'm happy with that.

Kamna's dorm residents and supervisors are more than satisfied with her performance. Her last year's evaluation highlighted several areas where her peers judged her to be exceptional. She was highly rated for being accessible, personable, outgoing, and a good listener. They applauded her programs as being relevant and informative, and they liked her enthusiasm.

What does she do to earn such applause? How does she go that extra step? Kamna attributes her success to never settling for the norm but instead always striving to do a little more than necessary. She cited this example: "One of an RA's responsibilities is to put on programs for the dorm. When we go through training, we are given a list of programs that are required such as drinking responsibilities, AIDS, acquaintance rape, etc.. I could have probably just gotten in the appropriate speakers and done the required programs. Well for me that's not quality work. I decided to survey the residents of my dorm to find out what they wanted to discuss in addition to the necessary topics. By taking that extra step I feel my customers - in this case, the residents - were pleased because they felt listened to.

Kamna cautioned about letting a job totally encompass you. She said, "Your job is probably going to be a big part of your life and identity but there might be a time when you leave that job for whatever reason. What are you going to do if you've failed to maintain other relationships, other hobbies, and other interests?" She feels maintaining other interests is essential for balance in her life which in turn contributes to her success and happiness. "When I'm happy with myself, I know that I'm leading a balanced life. Usually for me, that balance means doing the things I think are important such as helping other people, doing well in school and having some time for myself and friends. If I'm balanced, I can focus. If I am focused, I can do quality work.

Kamna revealed a time when the pressures from school and her job clouded her "focus" and almost got her in hot water. "One thing about being a resident advisor is, like any leader, you have an image and reputation to maintain. Last year, at about 11:30 one evening," Kamna related, "my partner and I were in my room. Mid-terms were just over, we were feeling the pressures of the job, and basically we were stressed out. Now when we took the job, the previous RA's had given us a box of stuff with all their files and a can of beer. The beer, they had said, was for a time when the stress of the job got to us. This was the day, we both agreed."

"Now, neither of us really liked beer but we decided we needed it. Although we enforce the no-alcohol policy and were both under 21, we agreed to do it. We stuffed a towel under the door, quietly opened the can, poured it, and took a little sip. Then the resident under us turned up his music really loud and I decided to go tell him to turn it down. He gave me a hard time and told me he was sure we couldn't hear it in our room. I told him to come on up and hear for himself. On the way up, I remembered the beer. To make matters worse, I had confronted him earlier for alcohol use. I started freaking out—my reputation was going to be destroyed. As it turned out, my partner heard us coming up and put the beer away. It just goes to show that as a leader you have an image to maintain. Sometimes it gets to be a pain, but that comes with the job."

Kamna has become an effective leader at a young age. And not without challenges. Kamna is legally blind!

Angle View 10
FOLD, SPINDLE...& BIND IT!
Romas- Marketing & Packaging Entrepreneur

"It's a good feeling; a very sound feeling," said Romas when asked about quality work. He continued, "The variables that pull that feeling together can change, but the feeling is always strong."

"Like everybody else, we put in enough hours. It is important for us to feel good about our work. When we feel that our work is 'OK' - that 'OK' is for us, high quality. We know that if the product or the relationship is not 'OK,' we don't get that good feeling."

That good feeling comes from over 25 years experience in marketing and packaging. A few years ago, Romas and his partner formed their own company that addresses the needs of everything that holds loose leaf. For a customer needing specialty binders, binder tabs, presentation folders, etc., Romas will find the right manufacturers to build the needed items.

Romas said quality was not always measured by financial success. "We don't necessarily feel good just because we may have made a lot of money one month or shipped a lot of orders. Quality work is more intrinsic. We look at things like how effectively we satisfied our customers, how efficiently we worked, how well we communicated with our manufacturers, and how promptly we addressed any problems. These things are important to a service oriented company like ours."

Producing a quality product doesn't always get the notice it may deserve. Romas can spend days or months with a client making the most detailed decisions and evaluations regarding a product. For example, a loose leaf binder: a lot of thought goes into deciding the ring size and type, the cover design, the script styles, the color for the lettering and the binder itself, and on and on. "The funny part about it," said Romas, "is that many times these things (binders, boxes, packaging) are immediately discarded by the ultimate consumer who has no idea what went into the production. People would be surprised if they knew the details of how much work goes into the actual fabrication of a package, whether it is a presentation folder or a box on a supermarket shelf. The dichotomy continues to amaze me; there's so much effort, time, and money put in only to have the consumer view it for a few seconds."

Romas adds that, "Nothing is saved; it is a very impermanent society. In our business we have to accept that all our efforts may go unnoticed or unappreciated."

Of course that reaction doesn't deter Romas. His goals for success include personal goals for quality and a good mesh of job and family. "Being in your own business is a wonderful place to be. They say never bring the office home but I don't subscribe to that. I feel you need your home as a kind of stabilizer. It reinforces the business side of your life. My business partner and I have a strength of conviction about the company. Our families feel good about it and the office feels good about it. There's a workable balance right there. You can't exclude one from the other."

The Angle on Chapter 5

In a sense,
each "angle" used for viewing
quality is a statement for diversity.
Jeremy Warren writes about weaving
a "mosaic" rather than turning everyone into
that salad we call a "melting pot." Diversity will
not go away. This chapter suggests taking some
time and energy and spending them very wisely on
awareness and understanding. After that, we can
move on to making real changes that scoop up
that extra value that comes with a
population full of valuable
resources.
RG

5

DIVERSITY, WORK TEAMS & QUALITY
Jeremy G. Warren

I believe that the Management of Diversity and Total Quality are closely linked in organizations of today and the future. I will go so far as saying that you cannot be a "Total Quality Organization" without attending to Management of Diversity. As you read this chapter it will become quite clear as to why my lenses see this inevitable marriage.

My initial belief is that the central theme of each is lodged in the values of an organization, which are in turn driven by the organization's culture. Thus, in making the management of diversity and total quality work; we must understand that we are first looking at cultural change. Cultural change is difficult as we all know; because in essence culture can be a barrier to the new state or value system that is being created. Thus, it is important to understand that changing culture and values is a process. As such, let's consider the following:

HERE'S A PATTERN TO FOLLOW

Commitment and support throughout the organization for this new state. Ownership for the new state must be accepted and lived out. Owners must walk their talk and the resources must be committed for the organization to get to the new state.

Organizational Development approach must be used. Those of you involved in total quality organizations know that training is only one piece of getting to the new state. Management of Diversity requires a similar approach. The values of the organization and its culture must be evaluated. Do they support and nurture the new state or are they a barrier? What is required is not incremental change but rather a paradigm shift. The faces of the workforce and consumers are changing. Just as there is a business rationale for organizations to embrace Total Quality, much of the same business rationale drives the need for organizations to effectively manage diversity.

Employee Involvement is required as well. Managing diversity in an organization is everyone's business. How and to what extent employees are involved in shaping the culture and values of an organization is directly proportional to their level of buy-in and support of sustaining the new environment.

Time and resources are a must! Many organizations do not understand the need for the commitment of time and resources. Organizational culture change is not achieved in six months. Policies, procedures, compensation, benefits, training and development, decision making, succession planning programs and processes must all be scrutinized. Do they support or hinder the new state? Organizations will be competing for the top talent in order to compete in a global economy. They will have to become "Employers of Choice." For many organizations, these changes will require time and resources.

WEDDING VOWS?

As we move forward with my premise of the marriage between Managing Diversity and Total Quality; it is important that we make distinctions between Managing Diversity, Valuing Differences, Affirmative Action, and E.E.O.

Affirmative Action and Equal Employment Opportunity are aspects of Title VII of the 1964 Civil Rights Legislation. Both Affirmative Action and Equal Employment Opportunity have a focus on numbers and both are supported by our judicial system. It is very important to understand how the reactions to Affirmative Action and E.E.O. have really shaped the thinking of many people in protected classes.

I recently observed a young African American male struggling with the issue of possibly acquiring a position with an organization because he was African American. The anxiety, rage, and ambiguity that he was feeling about having this position were all very painful to watch. His focus like that of many women, people of color, individuals with disabilities, etc., was on himself. That focus, on the job, translates into the person becoming a "Super Person," trying to do over and above the call of duty, a "Disenchanted Person," perceived as being very angry, a "Detached Person," aloof from parts of the organization; or a "Melter," a person who believes that he/she should give up significant aspects of their gender, sexual orientation, ethnicity or hide their disability to be accepted into the numerically dominant organizational culture. In any event, a significant portion of that person's energy is devoted towards nothing that supports the organization's mission. A lose-lose situation has developed for the person and the organization.

WHERE'S THE REAL FOCUS?

The question to be asked is whether his extreme focus on himself is properly directed. I say, categorically, NO! The much larger issue here is what does this say about the organization that puts itself in the position of being suspected of having to need to fill a position with a member of a protected class? It certainly says that historically the organization has probably not created an environment that has valued and fostered diversity. Therefore, if we accept this premise, we understand that the organization plays a major role. It must

75

analyze its promotional policies, employee development, evaluation, reward, succession planning, compensation, benefits, training and development systems, processes, and programs, and make the needed modifications. This requires an organizational approach very similar to the one used in Total Quality Management. We all know that customer service and meeting the requirements of the customer are what will make or break organizations in this new global economy. We also know that the workforce is rapidly changing with the increase of women and people of color as well as the effects of the Americans with Disabilities legislation on the workplace. So the burden of the focus must be on the organization while each person in the organization must be enabled to contribute as much of him or herself to the success of the organization as he or she can.

LAWYERS NOT NEEDED

Managing Diversity and Valuing Differences on the other hand have no legal or judicial ramifications. Valuing difference is an issue of the heart and requires individual courage. It requires us each to slow down our filtering systems and see people as individuals and to focus on the unique contributions that they bring as a result of being different from ourselves. We must try to understand and acknowledge In Groups vs. Out Groups and the relationship of power and value.

Managing Diversity is something that we have all done all of our lives. For example, we can think of our own relatives and how we deal with them individually when there is a gathering such as a family reunion. The slaves were managed from shore to ship to shore. We managed the Native Americans since the first settlers. The immigrants as they came on ships to New York were managed. While we may not like or agree with the way these groups of people were managed, the issue is that there is an influencing effect that valuing difference has on managing diversity. As we increase our capacity to value difference, we enhance our ability to Manage Diversity towards positive outcomes. The result is that in organizations we form a mosaic as opposed to a melting pot. My belief is that a "melting pot" requires individuals to sacrifice too much of what is unique to them; ethnicity, gender, disability or sexual orientation. In that case, a tension is produced that is counterproductive to the organization's effectiveness.

76

WORKING WITH BELIEF SYSTEMS

At the deepest level when you are speaking of valuing differences you are working with an individual's belief system. Changing the belief of an individual is a slow and frequently painful process. I believe that it is reasonable to expect that each person has his/her own limits as to how much he/she can or will modify their beliefs. Therefore, I believe that the focus on Managing Diversity and its business rationale is a more realistic focus for organizations as opposed to spending considerable resources on things such as sensitivity training, which after some point may not yield much return on investment. I agree that sensitivity is what enables us to speak of Americans with Disabilities as opposed to Handicapped, Native Americans as opposed to Indians, Sexual Orientation vs. Sexual Preference, etc.. However, I believe there is a balance and that organizations don't change until there is a "burning platform" underneath their feet. What they understand most is a business rationale. One may not change certain attitudes and beliefs, but one will probably respond to a business rationale.

The business rationale is clear when we look at Total Quality Management. As you know, many organizations have adopted some type of Quality Program as a way of doing more with less and improving quality in the products they produce or services they deliver. Many of these organizations have quickly discovered that the Total Quality Process is dynamic and that the quality of management and its decisions have improved. Also, the quality of work life of each individual member of the organization has improved as a direct result of being a "Quality Organization." The core worker begins to solve his/her problems or the team's problems. One of the beauties of the process is the buy-in and support that one gets for Total Quality Management from the top of the organization through to the bottom of the organization. Each person or team that receives work from another individual or team is viewed as a customer and the voice of the customer is heard and responded to as being valued (customers are viewed as internal and external to the organization). Valuing diversity then becomes crucial to valuing the voice of the customer.

I find the subject of TQM exciting because when one grasps the concept one quickly finds that TQM is a process, i.e., it has no definite ending. Managing diversity is much the same way because no matter how much work we do, we still have much more to do.

WHAT WAS HER NAME?

Let me give you an example: I recently had two Chinese women who were cousins, working for me, . They only slightly resembled each other and interacted very closely in their work responsibilities. Their names were Kathy and Mary. I never made a mistake and called Mary, Kathy, but I often have called Kathy by Mary's name. Every time I did this I would get very angry with myself. I am a person of color and this smacks of the very thing I have been a victim of—"They all look alike." I believe in my heart that I am not thinking "They all look alike" when I make this error, but why do I? After wondering what were Kathy's thoughts about my recurring mistake, I chose to discuss it with her. It was healthy for us to have the conversation; we both felt better and I haven't crossed their names since. Ah, the growth we experience when we confront our own shortcomings! I give this example because I want to enforce that there is so much to learn and work to do when Managing Diversity and valuing differences. There is no cookbook to which we can refer. It is a dynamic process, just as it is with TQM.

MAJOR CULTURAL CHANGE

Managing diversity and Total Quality Management are rooted in cultural change. No matter what process or author you use in Total Quality Management, the concept that it is about cultural change is generally accepted. Mission statements and vision statements are revisited and in many cases recreated. The point is that when you are talking about major cultural change, the top of the organization must be deeply involved and own the change. Thus, deep and intimate involvement from the top has become accepted as it relates to Total Quality Management. Organizations must pursue managing workplace diversity and valuing difference with the same passion, dedication, and enthusiasm. Ideally this would start at the top of the organization and must become a part of the organization's value system. Unlike affirmative action, where you did things because of the law, managing workplace diversity, which includes valuing differences, must become a core value of the organization. The customers' faces have changed. Whether you are in private industry, education or non-profit organizations, the demographic changes in this country have changed the faces of the customers.

BECOMING A GREAT ORGANIZATION

Are there other reasons for merging Managing Diversity and Total Quality Management? Total Quality Management is a strategic way of managing an organization. Management of Diversity must also be part of an organization's strategic plan. Organizations can die, survive, do well or be great. Becoming a great organization and sustaining that greatness require strategic planning. Total Quality Management with its focus on the "voice of the customer," internal as well as external, lays the groundwork for excellent strategic planning. We must remember that *internal customer* in Total Quality Management is defined as anyone who receives your work. Think of the impact on an organization that is made when the voices of all work teams are heard as succession plans are done for the organization. Succession plans that will shatter the "Glass Ceiling" for people of color, women, individuals of different sexual orientations, and the disabled. Managing Diversity becomes a value of the organization because it has support from all facets of the organization.

As organizations shrink, not only are they concerned about productivity and quality, but managing diversity as well. For people of color and the disabled, being laid off no longer means giving up the quest to crack the "Glass Ceiling." During a layoff they frequently become concerned about falling through the "Cellophane Floor." Opportunities for everyone are handled fairly when diversity is managed and valued.

The following model, developed by Dr. Ben Harrison, one of the nation's premier Diversity Consultants, and myself, depicts the similarities between the Total Quality and Managing Diversity models.

See model on next page.

79

THE CHANGE AND TRANSITION OF:

WORKPLACE DIVERSITY

STAGE 1- AWARENESS:
Presentation to Executive Leadership
Team- Removing the Confusion

STAGE 2- ASSESSMENT:
Executive Leadership Retreat:
• Impact of Demographics
• Leadership Willingness
• Corporate Vision
• Current Strategies
• Current Policies
• Current Structures

STAGE 3- DATA GATHERING:
Interviews, Focus Groups, Surveys
Data Analysis

STAGE 4- STRATEGIC PLANNING:
For Managing Diversity
For Valuing Differences

STAGE 5- DESIGN:
Process Design
Intervention Design

STAGE 6- IMPLEMENTATION:
Train Middle Managers
Train Internal Trainers
Train Internal Workforce

STAGE 7- CONTINUOUS IMPROVEMENT:
Maintain Original Focus/Vision
Accept Small Wins

TOTAL QUALITY

STAGE 1- PREPARATION:
Executive Management Training
Development of Corporate Strategy
Creation of Vision
Goals
Policy

STAGE 2- PLANNING:
Form Process Action Teams
Identify Support Systems
Identify Barriers to Success

STAGE 3- ASSESSMENT:
Individual
Organizational
Customers
Results Impact on Bottom Line

STAGE 4- IMPLEMENTATION:
Training of Managers
Train Internal Workforce
Maintain Executive Involvement
Maintain Tools for Success
Communicate Early Successes

STAGE 5- CONTINUOUS
IMPROVEMENT:
Maintain Original Focus/Vision

80

THE "WEAVE"

As you can see, the significant aspects of both models require complete organizational buy-in and support from top to bottom. Assessment, training and development, reward systems and follow-up are all requirements of both. My contention is that you cannot be a Total Quality Organization without also attending to the Management of Diversity issue as well. Dr. Harrison and I refer to the marriage of Total Quality and Workplace Diversity as "The Weave."

For those of you familiar with Total Quality Management or an Organizational Development approach to problem solving, you will recognize many similarities. They key is understanding the model, like a TQM model, is designed for <u>improving</u>! This is like self-actualizing; you are never done as you nurture the new state.

We must also remember this seven stage model for managing diversity gives time and opportunity for all employees to use all three speeds of learning and change. We all learn cognitively, behaviorally, and emotionally. When are values are up for personal review, the emotional learning is frequently the most difficult for us to move through. For instance, tomorrow you are transferred to another department in a different job. Your office is on the other end of the building. Your boss basically moved you over to the new job without much concern for your personal feelings about the move. You come in a different door each day behaviorally because it is closer to your office. But, you have emotional ties to the old job, the people, your title, and how you feel about the transfer.

NURTURING THE NEW STATE

My example may be fairly simple, but my point is that the emotional stuff takes time. Employees input the process and really work through some of their own personal issues at any of the seven stages. The more involvement at the beginning of the process by employees, the better the chances of making Managing Diversity an integral value of the organization.

However, the most important piece is the great need to see the management of workplace diversity as a process that requires organizational strategic planning. When I speak of this I mean:

Environmental Scanning- Looking at your current and future internal and external customers with regard to ethnicity, gender, disability, sexual orientation. Ask what the organization need to do to manage the varied needs of these customers.

Vision- Is both personal and strategic. It pulls people to work. It states what the values of the organization are and how they will be lived.

Mission- It speaks to the strategic thrust of the organization. Mission pushes the organization because from the mission come goals, objectives, and key opportunities which drive a team toward success.

Strategic Opportunities- As the strategic opportunities for an organization continue to present themselves, the diversity of the population demographics associated with the opportunities become omnipresent. Hence, the impact of Managing Diversity on the bottom-line. As we discussed earlier, Managing Diversity is part of the business rationale.

While assessment and training are key elements along with nurturing the new state, what is most important is understanding the commitment of the organization from the top. In this model, Managing Workplace Diversity becomes a strategic objective. The result is that there is hope for Managing Workplace Diversity to become part of the organizational culture. Everyone, as in Total Quality Management, becomes involved. Just as Total Quality Management organizations look for other Total Quality Management organizations when selecting vendors, the same phenomena can happen with organizations that do well with managing workplace diversity and valuing difference.

To this end, we will need transformational as well as transactional leadership with the former often being the initial owners and generators of change in our organization. This change will require courage from each individual in an organization; courage to try and courage to try again when we fail. Trust that when we fail we will be supported to live out our vision of a workplace that is congruent with the organization's mission.

POINTS TO REMEMBER/THINGS TO DO

1. Entrance into the global economy depends on customer service.
2. The global economy also demands meeting customer requirements. Don't move forward and backwards on this one.
3. Managing diversity helps with customer service.
4. Managing diversity and Total Quality are rooted in cultural change.
5. There are no definite endings to the TQM and diversity processes.
6. The top level of the organization must be deeply involved with cultural change.
7. Review and use the 7 stage model for managing diversity.
8. Diversity and work teams are components of empowerment.

Workforce Diversity Inventory

1. Recognize that each person has a different background, set of values, and a unique view of the world.
   DOING GREAT — JUST OK — IMPROVEMENT NEEDED

2. Talk to people from other cultures about their background, values, and principles. Get to know them!!
   DOING GREAT — JUST OK — IMPROVEMENT NEEDED

3. Recognize your own attitudes, biases, and stereotypes.
   DOING GREAT — JUST OK — IMPROVEMENT NEEDED

4. Think back to a time or situation where you were "different" and recall any fear, emotions or confusion.
   DOING GREAT — JUST OK — IMPROVEMENT NEEDED

5. Separate your expectations of each person from the stereotypes of each person's group.
   DOING GREAT — JUST OK — IMPROVEMENT NEEDED

6. Provide support and resources based on job-related and individual development needs...not on personal/group traits.
   DOING GREAT — JUST OK — IMPROVEMENT NEEDED

7. Set standards on job-related requirements.
   DOING GREAT — JUST OK — IMPROVEMENT NEEDED

8. Attribute success to effort and ability.
   DOING GREAT — JUST OK — IMPROVEMENT NEEDED

9. Attribute failure to lack of training, insufficient effort, and possibly poor resources, but not to low innate ability.
   DOING GREAT — JUST OK — IMPROVEMENT NEEDED

10. Never start, repeat or accept jokes or comments demeaning to people based on unchangeable traits or characteristics.
    DOING GREAT — JUST OK — IMPROVEMENT NEEDED

11. Find opportunities to celebrate the diversity of your work group.
    DOING GREAT — JUST OK — IMPROVEMENT NEEDED

12. Remember that a diverse workforce is the reality and how we manage it will determine our success.
    DOING GREAT — JUST OK — IMPROVEMENT NEEDED

Angle View 11
NO TRUCKS, BUT WE KEPT TRUCKIN'
Glenn - Trucking Company President

"I like to describe my job as similar to that of an orchestra leader. I don't specialize in anything, but I have to bring the entire staff together in a complete, harmonious situation. My job is to ensure the operation interrelates successfully."

Hand over the baton to Glenn, president of a mid-west trucking company he founded in the early 1980's. For Glenn, conducting his 300 member orchestra means meeting customer commitments, ensuring on-time delivery with damage free freight, and keeping competitive rates. A high quality performance is the only one he demands of himself.

"Our priority is with our customers. Our operating objectives are blended with customer expectations. When I finish a week and know that, as a company, we have met our objectives and those of our customers, then we have been successful."

Glenn's strategy is to stay away from the nitty-gritty details of running his company. "Everyday I meet with two or three department heads individually for about 30 minutes to review our "measurements listing" which outlines key operating concerns," he said. These reviews help keep things on track. But there's a limit to what I personally try to do. I don't try to force my staff. I want them to make decisions. I have found if I try to run everything, the smart ones will turn decisions back into my court."

"I have also learned that once a manager gets things going smoothly, it is not always necessary to keep hammering for improvements. I don't want to try to improve things more than I can reasonably expect."

Letting his staff have autonomy has helped Glenn keep a balanced perspective on his life. "For me, balance means not overdoing anything. I'm not a 60 hour a week guy. I have to have time to enjoy recreation, sports, entertainment, my wife, and my children. When it's time to back away from business, I go. Having this kind of balance is good for me, so I'm pretty sure it's good for the people around me. I can always be reached for emergencies, but I'm not always there."

Especially in the early days of the business, there were special customer challenges to overcome. Glenn found to be successful required creativity and cunning. "When I started the business we had four trucks and twenty trailers. Naturally, we went around knocking on doors to get contracts. I can remember going to one major company. The manager asked us how many trucks and trailers we had. We told him. He said that ordinarily he would never even talk with anyone with so small a fleet, but because we were a minority contractor, he'd grant us an interview. We didn't get the business."

"We learned a valuable lesson that day. The next time we knocked on a door, we said we had twenty-five trucks and one hundred trailers. Potential contractors still felt we were small, but not too small to talk with us. Essentially we had created a phantom fleet we could access with some footwork. The tactic worked. Afterward we developed a wonderful sales pitch, creating phantom fleets whenever needed. After getting a contract, we'd guarantee a start date in thirty days, and then we'd run out and buy or lease the equipment needed to fulfill the requirements."

For Glenn, attaining the highest quality marks comes from satisfying his customers and being "into people." "No matter how hard you try," he said, "I don't think you will reach your highest level if you are not able to work well with your customers and staff. You must relate to them, encourage them, and be there for them. When it comes to judging the quality of what you do, the customer is really the only one whose judgment counts."

Angle View 12
OOPS! GLASS ON THE FREEWAY!
Ed - Owner, Glass Shop

"The glass shook...bounced...and shattered over three lanes of the freeway!" Today, Ed works with glass. He does residential and commercial window replacement, door replacement, and the installation of other types of mirror and glass work. His background is in quality management. He had been quality manager for several high technology companies over the past 15 years. Before changing professions, Ed felt that he had internalized the key issues that make a customer "feel like coming back." He remarked that he was always learning and was surprised at how their needs and wants could change "in an instant." With a meditative look he mused, "You've got to be quick on your feet or they'll leave you behind."

"In this industry you have to make installs and repairs look as good as the originals with minimal hassle to the client." During the interview, Ed was working on a 2x6x8 foot table that was covered with a soft substance (indoor/outdoor carpet). "You need to work with glass on a soft and level surface." He told of times when he or a worker had not taken the time to prepare the surface, "glass slivers from a previous cut were imbedded in the table and we didn't take the time to prepare. It hurts when it scratches a new piece...and it's always the expensive stuff."

Ed felt strongly about balance. He said, "what helps keep some balance in my life is one rule I go by at work. Measure twice, cut once." He later whispered that on this particular day since he was talking while working, he's measuring three times! "Balance," he said, "means leaving each day with enough energy to be able to act decent with the people I'll be talking to that night. I try not to leave with nothing left." He went on to explain "when you leave, try to forget about it and think about something else. In the evening do things that give you a contrast from what you were doing in the day." His contrast to the physical labor was to read, go to movies and relax with the family.

Ed's phone rang a couple of times. He talked with a sub-contractor about a job installing commercial mirrors for a brand new store. He cautioned the person on the line to avoid a repeat of the freeway mess Ed had while rushing to a job. When he hung up, he was especially careful not to let the distractions create defects in the job he was completing. "Listen" he said, "that's what a cut sounds like. I save the old extra pieces so we don't have to charge the customer. Low scrap rates allow us to pass on the savings to the customer. One way or another, the customer has to pay for the scrap."

He went on to emphasize that success means taking into account the experience of the people that work for you. He never starts a job until everything is ready and the tools are gathered. He says, "Don't rush and double check the work that's done."

To be a good performer, Ed thinks that you have to sometimes be a monomaniac. He explained that this is a temporary state as you start a new project or purchase a new business. You have to have a mission that you're obsessed about for a period of time. He suggests that you get back to balance as soon as possible. "You have to have a lot of confidence in yourself, you also have to want a challenge and be able to implement changes in order to see results."

When asked about the freeway mess story he recalled, "I was rushing down through city streets to get to a job. I didn't have time to stop and check the load before getting on the freeway." Ed paused and laid down the tools he had been using. "I thought going slower would make up for my laziness. A light gust of wind caught the glass and it slowly began to shimmy. Next thing I knew a pocket of air picked it up and tossed it onto the freeway. I was horrified, but I learned my lesson."

Unfortunately, Ed the "glassmaker" passed away before publication of his comments and recommendations. We can all be assured that Ed lived by his beliefs in doing quality work and endeavoring to keep the balance in life. He's gone, but a part of him might live through his comments to us. This book is dedicated to his memory.

Angle View 13
THE CASE OF THE "GROWLING" COMPUTER
Bruce - Software Engineer and "Daddy"

"I can't believe I'm getting paid to have this much fun." About 12 years ago, Bruce completed his education in the humanities. He studied English, statistics, basic psychology, and educational psychology. He says he "fell into educational research" when he began working for a high technology firm in Mountain View, CA. He felt it would be difficult without a formal degree in computer science or electrical engineering, but he loved it so much the die was already cast.

Most of Bruce's duties include writing custom software for clients and doing contract programming. He says "the specific tasks almost always get extended." He says that people often don't really know what they want. They often ask if they can do this or that with a program and often focus on how to simply get the information out of the computer.

Bruce truly believes that the customer or user is king. "The machine is a tool that should be adaptable to you" he says. "There's nothing that can't be done with software" he continues. He's uncomfortable with the way many users have been treated..."they've been told that they can't do things the way they want to do them." He believes that the people who have the ideas are the people doing the work. Sure, he knows the technical side, but they know what it's supposed to do.

When asked about sustaining quality he says, "A high quality product is efficient, well-designed, performs the function it's intended to perform, and solves the problem...that's critical." "There are plenty of solutions in search of problems. Many miss the target—they just don't stop whatever hurts from hurting." It's tough he says because "it's not always clear." Bruce was doing the membership mailing list for a large chain of department stores. The system users proposed adjusting a complex two-report procedure. Bruce felt that this wasn't hitting the problem. The real issue was that the two reports got separated and the solution was to simply combine reports. When there were two reports they got lost in the stores. "It wouldn't have really solved the problem." "High quality

89

work has to solve the problem." He says identifying the real problem is at least as important as anything else you do.

His personal approach to quality is to quickly involve the user. He likes to get a quick prototype into their hands. "They can tell you right away by using the prototype." "You get info and users have their eyes opened." He says this is a tremendously rich interaction. "They're telling you what a high quality solution to the problem would be." He tells of a mix up in labeling a "terminal ID" at a credit card company. Something wasn't right so he checked with the user before continuing and thus avoided a $6 million mistake.

Bruce believes that balance does affect work performance. "In my life, balance takes a specific form. I love what I do, but I have to be careful. Otherwise I'll work too long and not be at my best during my personal time." "There are physical prices you pay for being out of balance." "Recently, I was at a client site, the weather was miserable and the commute was terrible. I picked up my young daughter and had to take a big breath and remember who I was dealing with." "After looking into her eyes," he continued, "I needed to remember what it's really all about. As much as I love my work it's not who I am. My relationships with other people—those are the most important things and that's really what I am, what it's all about, and that's what suffers when I'm out of balance."

Bruce keeps a sign above desk: Choose two—good, fast or cheap! He says "Often you can't implement the right solution but you use one that solves the problem based on the need for a quick solution." "If you're lucky you'll be able to go back and implement the right solution." He explains that sometimes solving the problem should take precedence over solving it in the right way. The tendency is to never like someone else's code, "but did it solve the problem?."

Bruce tells a couple of funny stories about mis-communication. He tells one story of the "growling" computer. "We got a call from a user saying 'my computer is mad at me, it said Grrrrrrr.' We had left the message in the software as a joke, figuring no one would ever see it...we were wrong." "They did find the message and thought the computer was angry because they had done something wrong."

In another case an employee said they didn't get their "numbers report," a report they weren't actually supposed to be getting. It turned out that the famous "numbers report" was a core dump (the program encounters an error, stops running and prints out everything it knows). They were filing it away. "I don't know how many filing cabinets they had filled."

When asked what he thinks people should do to perform well, Bruce gave four answers:

1. Ask yourself, am I willing to sign my name to it? It doesn't necessarily mean it's perfect...it means I've made my best effort.

2. Aim high, if you expect the best, you generally get it! This principle cuts across all levels. Staff and management want to excel, to do well. As long as you let them know what's expected they'll perform and probably beat your expectations. Give them the tools, support, advice and freedom. Stand back and let them do it.

3. Don't forget who you're working for. It's the user who is really your boss, who'll tell you when you've got it right and when you don't. It doesn't matter how good it is technically. Go to the people who understand the problem. Help them tell you. You won't like everything you hear.

4. Do something you like. My dad told me "it's three times as hard to do a good job when you don't like what you're doing."

The Angle on Chapter 6

Some
don't believe it
but the fields of television,
theatre, and film have a keen interest
in their "angle" on quality. Janice Edwards
takes us through an exciting overview from the
perspective of those who are successful in
their respective fields whether it's
on the air waves, the
stage or the big
screen.

6

QUALITY LIFE IN TELEVISION, FILM & THEATRE
Janice L. Edwards

"I try to make my ideas hard to resist. I'm not disappointed if they don't get it. My ideas about something don't change with rejection. If I think something is good, if I think something's in style, it never goes out of style for me." Kevin Costner

"Quality to me is something that appears to be crafted as opposed to just made. Something in which it's apparent that great care was taken." Stephanie Noonan-Drachkovitch

"You're dealing in Hollywood with a lot of lawyers, agents, and business managers who say, 'hey, you could be making so much more money if you took this job.' So, then the artist inside of me says, I'm not a whore, I can't just do it for the money." Robert Townsend.

WHO'LL DO THIS INTERVIEW?

A few years ago, information about a movie called American Flyers was sent to our office. It was a weekend assignment of interviews, an in-town junket, that did not appeal to either the co-host or to the older field producers. I was the only one who had a really strong feeling about doing it. So I asked to produce it. One of the principal actors was an easy-going affable man who brought his wife and young child with him. He gave a thoughtful interview. My piece was well received when it aired and months later, the executive producer boasted that we had snagged an interview with that actor, whose stature was growing as more of his pictures were released. The actor, now internationally known and father of three, was Kevin Costner.

When you look at quality work in television, film or theatre, quality, like beauty, is often in the eye of the beholder. In this chapter you will find out how the following people feel about quality work.

SOME REAL STARS!

Kevin Costner- film maker, actor, and director.

He has an international box office appeal that crosses gender lines. One source estimates that his gross movie earnings came in at more than $50 million dollars in one year. He received seven Academy Awards for "Dances With Wolves" in which he was director and star. His movie credits include "JFK," "Bull Durham," "The Untouchables," "Robinhood: Prince of Thieves," "Revenge," "American Flyers," "Silverado," "No Way Out," "Field of Dreams," "Fandango," "The Bodyguard," and "Perfect World." As president of his production company, TIG Productions, Kevin is continually developing projects.

Stephanie Noonan-Drachkovitch - Vice President of Programming, Group W. Broadcasting.

She has served as Director of Development for Buena Vista Productions, a division of the Walt Disney Company and as Vice-President and Chairman of 44 Blue Productions, a producer and distributor of syndicated specialty programs. She has worked as an

93

Executive Producer or Producer at WPVI-TV and WCAU-TV in Philadelphia, KATU-TV in Portland, KRON-TV in San Francisco, and Lorimar Telepictures in Los Angeles. Stephanie is also the author of <u>Mother Knows Best</u>, Ballantine Books.

Lloyd Richards - Tony Award winning director, Dean of Yale School of Drama.

He is a Tony Award winning director for the Broadway play "Fences"—one of his many collaborations with playwright August Wilson. A native of Toronto, Canada, Lloyd has acted and directed on and off Broadway and throughout the United States. He has served as the artistic director for the National Playwrights Conference of the Eugene O'Neil Theatre Center since 1968 and as President of the Society of Stage Directors and Choreographers. His many honors include one from the Writers Guild of America and the Yale Repertory Theatre's special Tony Award for Outstanding Regional Theatre.

Marlene Ryan - Actress, director, and talent coach.

She is a critically acclaimed and award winning actress who founded "A Class Act: Acting Company" and who created the unique A Class Act: Directing with Intimacy class in which an equal number of actors and directors collaborate on scenes and prepare for filming. A native of Detroit Michigan, who has performed all over the United States, Marlene is the author of An Actor's Workbook. She appeared in the Bronze Award-winning film, Stress Test, which was honored at the International Film and Video Festival in New York.. She also conducts Self-Esteem summer workshops for actors on the island of Oahu, Hawaii.

Lena Sullivan - Producer and Public Affairs Director, KPIX-TV

She is an Emmy Award winning producer whose credits include producer of KPIX-TV's "People are Talking," a daily talk show that aired for fourteen years in the San Francisco Bay Area, and "Bay Sunday," a weekly public affairs talk show. In addition to working as an associated producer and field producer on national and local shows including "PM Magazine," "Can This Marriage Be Saved?," and "The Afternoon Show," Sullivan has produced videos as an independent producer.

Robert Townsend - Film maker, actor, and director

His first film, the hit comedy, Hollywood Shuffle addressed the plight of African-American actors in Hollywood seeking to do work beyond stereotypical roles. This box-office hit catapulted the Chicago, Illinois native to international fame. The story of how he financed the first cut of the film on his credit cards became nearly as popular as the film. Townsend's other credits include producing, writing and acting in the popular HBO special "Partners in Crime", "Townsend Television", "The Five Heartbeats", and "The Meteor Man." He was the director of Eddie Murphy's film "Raw." His acting credits include "The Mighty Quinn", "A Soldiers Story", "Rat Boy", and "American Flyers." Townsend is president of his production company Tinsel Townsend Productions.

Evan White - Emmy and Peabody award winning investigative journalist.

His broadcasting career spans 35 years and he is an Emmy Award and Peabody Award winning journalist who has worked all over the United States. His reports and news documentaries have often been characterized by their controversial nature and have prompted others to respond and to take action. Since 1982, Evan has co-anchored KRON-TV's 5 pm newscast in San Francisco. He has received a Best Newswriting Award for Live at 5 from the Associated Press.

COMPARE THESE LISTS!

The means for evaluating quality work in these media could go on separate checklists:

List A
- Did we tell the story we intended to tell?
- Were our production values high?
- Did we meet or surpass our standards?
- Did we cover all the points we planned to address?

List B
- DID IT MAKE MONEY
- Did it grab the anticipated audience?
- Did a new audience discover it?
- Is it worth investing money and time to ensure that it makes a profit in the future?

Although many insist that list B is the only standard that counts in the industries of television, film, and theatre today, for those involved in the production of work for these media, List A is still the closer guideline for judging quality work. The bottom line, meaning profit or loss, is being emphasized as never before, and consideration of that affects which shows get on and stay on the air, which plays go up, and which films are made and which ones go straight to video.

I chose the people in this chapter because, through working with them, interviewing them or experiencing their work, their passion and commitment to quality had touched my life and the lives of many others. In any field, inspiration and dedication are essential elements in the production of work that surpasses median standards.

INTERNAL STANDARDS

In television, film and theatre, you are dealing with highly visible work. At an average theatre, your play will generally be seen by at least 250 people in one night. A low rating of just one point in television means that at least 22,000 people saw your work, and every filmmaker hopes his or her film will attract millions of patrons.

With even the smallest numbers, it is easy to understand why there is often disagreement on what meets the standards for quality work. If we are comparing lists A & B, your news programs may receive Emmy and Peabody awards but may not have the ratings and advertising dollars of a soft news program. Your play may receive Tony nominations and good reviews, yet it may not attract the volume of patrons that flock to a formulaic musical. Your film may win an award at the Cannes film festival and never show a profit at the box office. Everything on list A checks out, but you fail at question one on list B which is, did it make money?

WHERE'S THE CONTROL?

Most times there is an internal sense that lets you know you have done your best work and have mastered all factors within your control. The collaborative nature of the work means there are always certain factors over which you will not have control. But, in the best case scenarios, your colleagues share your values and all are synchronized. Ideally, you have had time to research and prepare, to insure that your message is being communicated as you desire. And upon later review, after the flush of meeting your deadline, you still feel confident that the elements came together in a way in which you can be proud.

When I first started producing stories for a local television station, one of my first pieces was in recognition of the late Dr. Martin Luther King, Jr.'s birthday. I decided to use footage from Civil Rights marches, sit-ins, arrests, and moments of triumph set to Stevie Wonder's "Happy Birthday (To You)," commemorating Dr. King's birthday. The piece ended with a portion of Dr. King's "I Have A Dream" speech. I used no voice-over (narration) from the co-hosts of the show, feeling that the pictures, words, and music were more powerful without it. In the editing room, the editor had trouble cutting one section on the right beats of music. We spent nearly 30 minutes trying to get that one part right. The editor tried to persuade me that few would notice that it was off, but to me, it was a glaringly discordant note in an otherwise harmonious piece. Finally, after another 15 minutes, but still before air time, it was just right! We were both moved and pleased. I knew I had done my personal best and as I looked at the story again, I felt I had achieved my goal. Later when we received several calls and letters from viewers who had appreciated the piece, I had external reinforcement that matched the internal knowledge that I had met my own standard of quality.

EDITING 6 COMMERCIALS

A few years later, a business partner and I were editing the last of six commercials for a television special. We had been editing the spots for several long days and, on this day, we'd been going for eighteen hours straight. Any excuse to escape that editing suite would have sounded great, but we knew we couldn't face ourselves if we let fatigue color our judgment. An hour and a half later, all the pieces worked. Our work was done...well! We were satisfied and when we finally slept, we slept well.

Stephanie Noonan-Drachkovitch concurs that time is a big factor in achieving high quality work. "I try to personally achieve it by having enough time to devote to pay attention to the detail that's required. I think attention to detail really is probably the most important thing."

How does news anchor and reporter Evan White know when he has done a good job?

"Me, I like to kick a little butt and I hope a story shakes something. But that is not the only definition of quality, not every story has to do that...I feel if I went out and in two to three minutes was basically able to take something I thought was important and was able to translate it into some form of storytelling that was effective in reaching people...then I was successful."

WHEN I'M TOUCHED

As a producer of a talk show, Lena Sullivan feels she has done high quality work when 1) she has created a positive environment for her staff and things are in order, 2) she has enough time to focus on her own responsibilities, and 3) her personal life is in balance. She thinks that talk show hosts Oprah Winfrey and Phil Donahue generally do high quality work, but she has a litmus test for evaluating anything she sees on television.

"When I am touched by a story and it grabs my heart and I forget my television background and watch as a viewer—when I become so involved with the program that I don't even look at the technical aspect. When I watch anything, when I read anything, when I listen to people talk, my automatic reaction is—is there a story here? So when I can completely lose that and become the viewer, then what was done worked."

Kevin Costner has his own test for movies. "I'll tell you what happens when I see a really good movie—two things always strike me—one, that I wish I was a part of it and second, if it's really quality work, I often don't know how they did it. You admire it so much that you realize that you wouldn't have known how to do that, 'cause it's very smart'."

For Robert Townsend, a commitment to quality work has meant more personal scrutiny.

"For an actor, it's trying to be believable in different moments and being very creative in those moments. As a director, it's coming up with great pictures and incredible compositions that the actors can flow in and flow out of, creating three dimensional, four dimensional pictures. So there's different levels. For me, all levels (involve) trying to come up with quality. I discovered as I work on my craft, that it really comes from within Robert, too. I've got to improve me. My things, my shortcomings, whatever. I've got to work on those things because you can't live a certain thing on screen and not be it off screen."

The assessment for the internal guide is not only a personal standard, but also a work standard derived from observation of how the work can be done and from consideration of how one personally likes for it to be done. It is based on observable results - a deadline was met, an image was conveyed, a tangible product that embodied certain values was produced.

WAR - HOSTAGE - EARTHQUAKE

It is always gratifying to have your internal guidelines validated, and one way of increasing the probability of that happening is to constantly update the information you have. You must not only know what is being done, but also what has been done. Research or "homework" is essential in any field today.

On the news, whether the crisis is the outbreak of war, a hostage situation, an unstoppable fire or a 7.1 earthquake, a journalist has to trust that 1) the research done before, 2) the expertise acquired, and 3) the ability to comprehend, analyze, and disseminate new information, will all come together in minutes or even hours of incredible pressure. When advising journalists, Evan White counsels "You have got to go out and learn your craft. Look to people who you think do quality work and learn from them."

On a talk show, the producer and host(s) must trust that their collaboration, research, and agreement regarding the handling of any topic will support the free flowing exchange with the guests, and leave them reasonably prepared for "bombshell" revelations—a guest walking off the set or surprise drop-ins. When it comes to in-studio melees, which have become more frequent as more talk shows enter the market (e.g. the fight on the Geraldo Rivera show), most are not well-prepared for outbreaks, although you can often predict who might initiate a conflict.

With film, a filmmaker controls all the elements he or she can in pre-production, on location, and post-production. In a play, actors and director rehearse to discover the moments of wonder as well as to master the potentially bumpy moments. The research and preparation allow for the possibility or surrender to "live" unscripted moments that can inform or move an audience. As Marlene Ryan says, "High quality work in acting is discipline, which creates freedom, management which creates freedom, collaboration and cooperation which create freedom."

HOSTING A TALK SHOW

When I began hosting a talk show, I looked at the talk show hosts who had qualities that I admired. I also considered the professional and personal goals of my show. Empathy was important—truly listening to, and assisting a rape victim, homeless person or battered woman in becoming comfortable sharing her or his story, without it seeming exploitive.

Research and homework included watching the forerunners, watching my own tapes to correct habits that did not serve me, and to identify internal discomforts that I had to resolve. When guests confided that my manner had put them at ease or viewers said the interviews had been interesting and thorough, I knew my research had paid off.

Research is one crucial element for reinforcement of internal standards. Another is the attitude that you are the president of your own company regardless of your "true" position on any project. What this means is that at whatever level you are working, you recognize your responsibility and accountability for a certain percentage of the results. Robert Townsend gave his career a great boost when he found the means to finance his own film. He saw that he and many of his friends were not being offered the kinds of roles they desired, so he made a film "Hollywood Shuffle" that addressed his concern and also served as a resumé reel for his colleagues. He had done personal research and then acted as chief executive officer of his career by casting and directing himself. He is now president of his own Tinsel Townsend Productions.

Marlene Ryan is a staunch believer in actors creating their venues and not waiting around for the call from the casting agent or director. "(The safe route is) sitting by the phone and waiting for someone to give you a call as opposed to reading a book about a person that you think is fascinating—taking that material and transforming it into a vehicle that you yourself can perform. Waiting is like saying that if you're a writer, you're dependent on the publisher, and if you look at history, writing happened way before there was publishing—acting happened way before there was a film company or an agent.

Marlene adds to her idea of creating venues, "I often recall a wonderful woman who inspired me. She gets a wonderful idea for a piece, rents a room, and then charges everyone from five to fifteen dollars—she just does it!

THE ELDERLY AND DISABLED

Evan White's specialty as a news anchor and reporter is investigation of the problems that the elderly and the disabled face. It is his belief that journalists have a responsibility to represent those who do not have access to certain services. He thus, combines his internal standards with his investigative skills and knowledge.

"You've got to be on the lookout for people who don't have easy access—without your help for getting a message out that they're in need—they're in trouble. You need to be a watchdog in relation to government and other agencies that are supposed to have responsibility for public welfare and sometimes abuse it. There is a tendency to forget what our primary mission may be because more and more people are getting into the business who are in the entertainment-oriented mentality, not journalism-oriented mentality. The bucks are very big, so criteria are getting skewed. Establish your own style; your own criteria, your own list of what you think is important to make you proud of what you do and stick to it as best you can. You answer to yourself first; you have to."

Kevin Costner was president of the company when directing "Dances with Wolves" and he was very certain of the vision that he wanted to execute. "On Dances, I didn't need anybody to tell me if a scene didn't work. I could tell. We have a thing called dailies, where you look at the film you shot the night before. There were

days when I would feel terrific and days I would feel like a complete
amateur. And so, one reason why I was independent was I didn't
feel the need to be around a whole bunch of people telling me when
it didn't look great, because I knew that. It's just a conversation that
I didn't need to have because I can see when something is bad and
not good, I can be responsible for it."

DISCOVERING AN ACTOR'S STRENGTHS

Lloyd Richards says, "My process of work is one of suggestion,
gentle provocation, to ultimately arrive at that point where the actor
himself selects to do exactly what I want him to do so it is his...it is
not my imposition on him. I want the actor himself to discover
various strengths...and the consequence to be his choice from my
vision."

The challenge is to create, collaborate, and communicate with a trust
that there is an agreement on basic work ethics and standards and to
be willing to stand your ground and fight for what you believe in
when there are disagreements about those standards. This is not
advocating contentiousness—it is important to choose your battles
and to know the difference between s battle and a war.

"Fight against those forces that try to compromise you—whatever
they are—in the editing room, in the shooting, in management, in
producers, in co-workers. You've got to set your standard of what
you think is quality. There will always be attempts to compromise
you, and it's very easy to get into those attempts. It can cost you
jobs." - Evan White

"A person has to have high self-esteem to do well in television
because mistakes, when you make mistakes, are often recognized;
you're often criticized while good work is taken for granted. You
need initiative and assertiveness without being obnoxious...you
have to let people know you're there, because if you are not
assertive, you can be ignored." - Lena Sullivan

Once you have an ability to assess quality work based on internal
standards, supported by research and the attitude that you are highly
accountable, it is easier to put the external standards in perspective.

MONEY AND EXTERNAL STANDARDS

There is no doubt that money has always been an important consideration in television, film, and theatre, but the extent to which the bottom line affects what you see is constantly expanding. More action movies are made because they translate better than love stories on the international market. Television shows have plots revolving around hospitals or prisons to save on location expenses. News shows incorporate shots from video press kits in a story because it saves a crew the expense of shooting it. Theatres have an entire season of plays of one or two person shows. You can be sure that money is a primary consideration. When corporations become owners of film companies, consideration of whether a movie's audience is like the desired customer and decisions about which products will be seen on screen come into play. Product position is seldom subtle. At a recent symposium, high school students complained that product displays in movies are often longer than the commercials.

Directors dedicate their careers to the "director's franchise," making sequels to box office hits and putting aside films they long to make, due to the bottom line. News directors and general managers of stations are often chosen from sales and marketing departments; often the result is not a comprehensive view of news at the local, national, and international level, but the most palatable news that a target audience wanted to see and hear. What this means in terms of quality work is that when you consider lists A and B, your work will be affected by list B, whether or not you personally make the money decisions.

REMEMBER THESE?

List A
- Did we tell the story we intended to tell?
- Were our production values high?
- Did we meet or surpass our standards?
- Did we cover all the points we planned to address?

List B
- DID IT MAKE MONEY
- Did it grab the anticipated audience?
- Did a new audience discover it?
- Is it worth investing money and time to ensure that it makes a profit in the future?

Lena Sullivan says, "Creativity is not as much a priority, especially if it costs big bucks and the return is not there. I think bottom line is number one priority, bottom line is number two priority, and number three. There's a shift from a people friendly medium. Now employees are referred to as units of expense. Literally. I've heard the same term used in corporate situations for years, but it's one that is becoming more and more common in broadcasting. We are now units of expense. So that takes the human element out of it."

Stephanie Noonan-Drachkovitch adds her assessment. "The dollar drives the market -it's all the advertising dollar, so you just look at all the "quality" shows that have been canceled and look at the shows that have stayed on that have production values or storylines that aren't as deep or important or well written...The audience has found them faster than they've found other things. "There's a lot of reason why shows don't get ratings and they don't always have to do with quality. They really don't."

"At a certain point, we were having tremendous trouble with the wolf in "Dances with Wolves" and I had to make a decision. It cost me over ten days just working with him and it cost me a lot of money, but he was the namesake of the movie. So, while there were those around me who says, 'look, we've got to move on,' I realized how important the wolf was in the movie and you have to make those decisions."

"At the same time, you have to make those kind of decisions of 'look, we've stayed on that close-up long enough, we've got to move on. You have to be a realist in this world and I believe that you can be an artist at the same time." Kevin Costner.

We are looking at work in industries where it is extremely unlikely that you will spend the majority of your life with one organization or company. Of course, due to the changes in the global economy and many core industries, the whole concept of working an entire lifetime in only one industry has changed and fewer companies even offer the promise of lifetime employment.

Careers in film, theatre, and television have always been considered difficult to start, and challenging to maintain. Economic changes have only increased that perception and the reality.

THE SHOW'S BEEN CANCELED

I was shocked when I learned that the first television show for which I had ever worked would be canceled. I was stunned not only because we were all going to be laid-off, but also because my co-workers told me I was lucky to have worked for one show for three years when starting out. In the years since, I have worked for a number of national and local shows, and I now fully understand my former co-workers' attitudes. I also learned not to take cancellations personally and to understand that doing quality work is no guarantee of a show's survival. However, it is still necessary to look at the external signs for feedback - you have to determine if the audience that you did reach was the one you sought and identify what worked well and what did not, so that you may fine tune your work. While one particular job may end, the career is a dynamic and viable entity that will hopefully continue for a lifetime. Change does not mean failure- it is a part of the process. When Robert Townsend's second film, "The Five Heartbeats" was released, it did not match the box-office success of his first film, "Hollywood Shuffle." Robert offers his perspective on dealing with external criticism despite having met his internal standards.

"For every critic who hated the movie, there were people who said, 'I saw the movie five, six, seven times'—so when you have stuff like that going on, it just fills you. When you get Luther Vandross and Anita Baker calling, all these great artists going 'That movie touched me.' And then you go 'Ya'll are the music people: you're the hardest critics'—Then it's another kind of feeling. Part of it is, when you have a different vision, it's not embraced because you're going against the grain. If I would have come out with a drug picture with a lot of rap music and used rappers in different parts, then I would have had a hit movie. I'm not dealing with stereotypes, And you know, your battle is going to be a little bit harder. If I did what everybody else is doing, then , I'd make a lot more money, but I don't want to be a fad. I really see the arts as a spring board for social change, that's why I'm in it, to entertain people, hopefully to say something that will make people think. I've learned a lot, so going into my next film I'll know exactly how I want it to look, taste, and smell."

At the time of my interview with Lena Sullivan, "People Are Talking" was facing rumors of cancellation, and since our interview, the show has gone off the air. She shared her thoughts about that possibility.

A POWERFUL WOMAN

"I know that we're up against a major challenge being opposite the most powerful woman in television (Oprah Winfrey). Since I've been the producer here, we've gained one rating point, yet I know that the people making the decision (about keeping the show on) are not going to take that into consideration. But I feel good because I see how hard our staff is working—I know they are here late at night. I know that we explore different show ideas when topics come up that might be questionable, we talk about them, do we want to exploit it? I know that there is genuine caring and a genuine interest. I don't see it (cancellation) as failure, I really don't."

When my father decided to leave his law practice to teach instead, he advised me that the best way of achieving personal and financial success was to "Do something that you love, that you would get up in the morning and do, whether you got paid or not." Being well-paid is an important element in the rewards for quality work and the thought of high salaries attracts many to the fields discussed, yet—for most with longevity—creative fulfillment is the final bottom line.

Lloyd Richards recalls obstacles that prevented him from doing quality work.

"There was a point when I was directing a Broadway show where I may have chosen scripts for the wrong reasons. I did it because there was financial gain involved. You know, it's blood no matter what it is. The demands—on one's own involvement, engagement and self-utilization—are the same, whether it is a really good piece of material or a mediocre piece. And so, it's blood, whatever it is. It's shedding that for the right reasons, something you care about, even though the thing you care about and may do, may be even less developed than something else which is more secure. I've got to do the things that keep me in the theatre. I didn't come into the theatre to make money not that I can't use it, won't use it or that I don't want it, I don't mean that, but it was not the compelling reason."

COFFEE, POPCORN AND...BALANCE?

We have examined how internal and external standards, and research play a role in quality work in television, film, and theatre. The last critical element is balance. It is because of this factor that we titled this chapter "Quality Life" as opposed to "Quality Work." For most people in these fields, the idea of an eight hour day is a foreign concept. You work on a story or show until it's at its best possible level given your time constraints: you rehearse and rework a play as many hours as possible before opening night, you commit cast and crew to overtime, both in production and post production to make the best film you can. Yet, despite the demands and the inevitable dinners of microwave popcorn and coffee (if there's even time for that), most people seek a full life and work to maintain the personally fulfilling aspects of life beyond their jobs. They have learned that ultimately, personal satisfaction enhances creativity rather than detracts from it.

When I started working in television, there were months when it seemed I only used my apartment to shower, change clothes, and sleep. The satisfaction I derived from my work was exhilarating. However, I noticed that if I went too long without some private time, and time with family and friends, my level of satisfaction with my work decreased dramatically. Whether it's a film, television project or a play, each requires a different pacing, but all require a general level of care for my spirit, my mind, and my body that make it easier to do my best work. It is a privilege to do work I love. That combined with the appreciation of what it takes to cultivate a career allow me to savor my successes in a deeper way. My faith, family, and friends provide the critical balance for me.

Despite the necessity of putting other activities on hold at different times, after periods of incredible intensity and some 22 hour work days, most of us have learned to rejuvenate and to maintain the quality of life that we value. For Evan White, this is a new perspective.
"All my life, the work was my life and there was nothing else to it. My family suffered for that. I'm not that way anymore. My personal life is now equally important to me as my professional life and I just finally reached a balance. Also, I'm with a lady that's in the business and that helps me."

Stephanie Noonan-Drachkovitch, a married mother of three sons, says her life was "a thousand times easier" when she was single, but she adds that having a family definitely puts things in perspective.

"I think it helps you in terms of the quality of your work, it broadens your view of the world and it allows you not to take things so seriously that it can work against you. When I was single, I didn't have to care about how late I stayed at the office—work was my life. I didn't have anybody to go home to, so it didn't bother me to get in at the crack of dawn and leave when the sun went down. Having a family helps you in terms of the quality of your work. It broadens your view of the world."

Lena Sullivan concurs:
"Balance in my personal life means that there is enough time for family, friends, social commitments, and church. When all of that is in sync., then my work performance is greatly enhanced. When my work overlaps into my personal life then I don't think I perform as well because I'm not a workaholic. I'm much more objective when my personal life is in sync."

Lloyd Richards, who has been married for 34 years, knew that the odds against a stable life in his profession were high.

"I wanted to be married and stay married. Being in the business I was in I knew it was difficult to attempt to raise a family and be in the theatre looking for work constantly. My own sense of responsibility meant, that if I was having trouble finding work, and I had a family, I would probably get out of the theatre and get a job somewhere. So, I delayed getting married. I got concerned that we'd be able to raise a family and still stay in the theatre, which we have fortunately been able to do, and I consider myself very lucky in that regard."

For Robert Townsend, marriage and the birth of his children have heightened his creativity, helped him relax, and amplified his vision as an artist.

"To really be an artist, you've got to live life. You can't say, well all I want to do is make movies, you've got to go to picnics, the amusement park, and hang out with just regular people and enjoy it. I have the madness of my world as a director and writer, and dealing with studios, then I get to come home and just have fun, just be silly and stupid—and my wife is great! To understand what happiness is, you've got to be happy."

Marlene Ryan, happily married to her second husband for ten years, adds: "Balance is seeing that it's not all about work, that without play, my work suffers. It's friendships that are deep—people who hold me accountable for my words and actions—taking responsibility for my child in teaching him how to nurture himself. Balance means when I get into bed at night and perhaps I've just made love to my darling husband, and he's made love back to me, and everything is hunky dory—all bills are paid, everything is fine, I've created my butt off. I pull up those covers over me and I say "God what a day! That's it...that's happiness."

POINTS TO REMEMBER/THINGS TO DO

1. Celebrities often struggle to keep a focus on quality.
2. Be aware of your internal and external standards.
3. Some professions require a perfection standard most of the time.
4. Carefully select where you apply time for perfection. It always requires taking time from something else.
5. Create a positive environment for staff members.
6. Time spent on good research pays healthy dividends.
7. Specialized industries also require personal equilibrium and life balance. Avoid "Tantalus" on this one too!
8. Don't take yourself so seriously that it harms you.

Reward System Inventory

Team leaders and members can take this inventory to get a sense of the reward system in place within the group.

Scoring: 1 = lowest, disagree, 3 = average, 5 = highest, agree

1. We have a current and effective reward system.
      1   2   3   4   5

2. Preventive efforts and results get more attention than "crisis" management.
      1   2   3   4   5

3. Our focus is longer term rather than short term.
      1   2   3   4   5

4. Other co-workers and departments have input into our reward system.
      1   2   3   4   5

5. We reward performance that is accurately measured.
      1   2   3   4   5

6. Our reward system receives comments and suggestions that are primarily positive .
      1   2   3   4   5

7. We reward group projects and success more than individual effort.
      1   2   3   4   5

8. We avoid going overboard with too many posters, photos, slogans, etc.
      1   2   3   4   5

9. Our program leads to better products and services.
      1   2   3   4   5

10. Our program leads to satisfied repeat customers.
      1   2   3   4   5

TOTAL REWARD SYSTEM SCORE _____

Angle View 14
DO IT WITH YOUR BARE FEET!
Mark - Professional Waterskier

Mark is a professional waterskier. He is part of a team of performers who entertain audiences at a large popular west coast entertainment park. As part of his job he performs water ski, jet ski, and hang glider stunts. He has 20 years of experience as a waterskier and seven as a paid professional.

"A good day for me is when I'm consistent. That's what I strive for. After consistency, to take the quality higher, I want perfect form and execution of the stunts. It's like an ice skater or gymnast, I feel my best when I really 'nail' a trick."

The training for Mark's job requires years of practice as well as regular mental and physical preparation. Mark added, "I work out everyday. For me working out means mainly stretching, but I must do it to keep from getting injuries. To prepare for the stunts, I use a lot of mental imagery. I think about each new trick a lot and try to imagine in my mind the moves needed to complete it. After a while most tricks get to be habit. But there are always tons and tons of new tricks to learn and that's what keeps it fresh. If I were to get to a certain level and plateau out, I'd become stagnant and it wouldn't be as much fun. Every season I try to work on something new."

In addition to the personal preparation, the size and quality of the crowd can affect Mark's performance. He added, "The audience plays a big role in the success of the show. If only a few people show up it's hard to perform. A large crowd that's really noisy inspires us. I feel we all try a little bit harder then. The louder the crowd, the better the water stunt shows become.

"I feel lousy if I mess up but sometimes when the crowd cheers us on even more, it really helps to have the support. Sometimes the audience doesn't even know when we've messed up. Then we try to play it off and be a showman. For example, if we fall or mess up, we should keep smiling and never slap the water.

"Also, the crowd helps us with the comedy. In the beginning of the season some of the comedy isn't written into the show and we ad lib. The audience's response helps determine what we'll

111

keep. Sometimes even a mistake ends up as part of the show because the audience loved it."

One mistake that did not get included happened to Mark recently. This, one could say, was a day when everything went wrong. Mark shook his head before he went on. "I was doing the back barefoot act. I was trying something new before I left the dock and I fell on the step-off. We had to repeat it. Normally we just repeat it once but the second time I fell before the end of the course. At that point I was just going to go in and wait for the next act to start. The next act was a chase with jet skis. The guy who was supposed to make a pass on the jet skis couldn't get his jet ski to start. To compound things, he's deaf so it was hard for me to communicate with him from so far away. So I figured I'd go again and by that time he would be ready to go. Just as I was starting to go again, the ladies who were supposed to chase the jet skier had already started and were driving through the show course. They were chasing no one and I was skiing in the opposite direction - the jet skier was still nowhere in sight. It was a mess. The announcer was even stumped. He can only use so much 'fill' and then he loses it after a while."

Mistakes not withstanding, Mark loves the work. He said he stays with it because he enjoys the challenges, is always learning new stunts to incorporate in the shows and he likes the interesting people he meets on the job. He concluded, "If you don't like what you're doing, get out. You've got to be happy in your work to do well."

Angle View 15
NO YELLING, OR HOLLERING...
JUST "SCREAMING!"
Cheryl - Professional Screamer

Anyone who has been around an average two-or three year-old knows what a "screamer" is. Some toddlers can "belt 'em out" with abandon and send chills up any nearby adults' spines. Reprimanding them may not be the best course; they may be on their way to a career like Cheryl's. Cheryl is a professional screamer. That's right, she gets paid to scream. In fact as far as she knows, she is the only full time professional screamer in the country. And her "training," started, you guessed it, as a youngster.

"I've always enjoyed screaming, from the time I was a very small child. My mother was interviewed about my job and she said that's just the kind of child I was. The way I reacted to things, to anger, to frustration, to excitement, was to scream."

First, to clarify Cheryl's talent, screaming doesn't involve words; yelling and hollering do. Screams are simply gut wrenching cries and Cheryl has perfected every type imaginable. "I do all different kinds of screams," said Cheryl. "Everybody's favorite is the primal scream. I do different kinds of primal screams. I also do screams that start low and get loud, some that start loud and get low, some that waver in the middle, and some that waver at the end. Another favorite, but it takes some special effects, is the falling off the cliff scream."

Her talent is in demand. Cheryl has an album of screams and has screamed in about 40 films. Actresses, while talented in their own ways, often can't really scream. So Cheryl steps in and dubs over the actress' motions. Don't look for her name in the credits though. Screamers don't get credits and screamers don't tell whose vocals weren't up-to-snuff.

In this profession, like any other, there is a standard of perfection. Cheryl sets high standards for herself and says she can "feel" a truly great scream. "I can tell immediately when I've done a good scream. I can't hear myself as much as I feel it. There's a feeling of completion. It's a complete body experience from head to toe. There's a total release when I'm finished. "

Screaming, for Cheryl, is a very serious occupation. She has a clear cut approach to giving quality performances. It involves complete relaxation and rigorous mental conditioning. She said, "I have a natural talent but when I was young I really didn't know what to do with it. After my first job I was hoarse. I realized later that I had to practice and work to develop my screams. I learned quickly that to do a good scream I had to learn how to concentrate and shut everything out so I could totally relax. I do a lot of relaxation exercises. I really believe in clearing the mind. If my body is not totally relaxed when I do a very loud scream, I can not only harm my voice but also the muscles and ligaments in my back and chest. Total relaxation is critical for me."

To completely relax, Cheryl finds her life must be in balance. She says if she is tired or troubled by events in her personal life, she can't scream well. She tried once and learned how personal conflicts could interfere with a good scream. Cheryl went to an important job days after her grandmother had died. She said she found it extremely difficult to concentrate enough to get into a truly relaxed state of mind. She did not scream well, and pulled a muscle in her back. She wished she had just canceled the booking. Cheryl's advice: "If the goal is to do your best, don't do it at all if you're not going to be fully committed."

Her other advice is to be careful where you scream, especially if you aspire to greatness. Cheryl doesn't practice screaming at home; she prefers a car on an open road (windows rolled up tight of course). She also has found screaming, even at auditions, can be scary. One day the police arrived on the scene of an audition when frightened people in the next room thought a murder was taking place. It's all in a day's work for Cheryl.

Cheryl's lucky, screaming is a passion for her and she actually gets paid to do it. She says she's living proof that when you enjoy something, with some diligence, you should be able to turn your passion into an income. And no matter what you do, Cheryl stresses taking the time to concentrate. "When I can concentrate and relax, I think clearer, I act more swiftly, and I scream better."

Angle View 16
"TELL US A STORY...PLEASE!"
Diane - Professional Storyteller

There's magic in the air when Diane is performing. She captivates her audiences from the very young through the very young-at-heart. She makes them laugh, makes them cry, makes them quiver on the edge of their seats. Diane is a professional storyteller. She has a unique talent for bringing folklore alive and for creating new tales that she spins from her own experiences and history. Her skill lies in her voice, her gestures, and her ability to take herself and her audience into a world where, for the moment, fantasy becomes real and reality merges into fantasy.

Estimates vary, but according to the National Association for the Preservation and Perpetuation of Storytelling, there are approximately 200 people in the United States whose only or primary occupation is storytelling. About 40 or 50, like Diane imbue some of their stories with their rich African-American heritage. Most people may know about librarians or teachers who tell stories, but obviously few have encountered professionals in the field. "Adults ask me what I do for a living and I say I'm a storyteller. They look puzzled and restate their question asking 'What is your job?' They don't get it. That's funny to me. Even children aren't used to it. They'll ask me if I'm going to read to them. I say no, the stories are in my head."

Diane took a risk a few years ago when she decided to leave her job of 17 years to become a storyteller. Although she had been honing her skills part-time for over seven years, she still felt it risky to try to make it as a professional but she loved the work. For Diane it is important, if at all possible, to have a job you can enjoy. "The majority of people I know don't like what they are doing. Sometimes they have to deal with that in order to eat and keep a roof over their heads. Only a few are lucky enough to actually like what they do. If you see an opportunity and have the resources or backing to take a risk, try it. It might require some sacrifice to do something you really love."

To keep at the top of her profession, Diane says she practices, practices and practices some more. Her family, especially her two teenage children, have heard her stories many times and in fact have grown to love both storytelling and reading as a result. Also to do well in her profession, Diane stressed the need to be in tune with the child inside and not afraid to just let go of yourself. She said, "When I do storytelling, especially certain characters, Diane is gone." She continued, "You also have to be able to see the picture, see what you are telling. If I don't see the house, the character, the image, it's hard for me to tell it. If it's not real to me, it's not real to my audience."

Storytelling is a give and take experience. A good storyteller relies upon her audiences' reactions to determine the suitable embellishments that bring the stories alive. "Storytelling is like a bridge," said Diane. "It connects the teller with the audience. I do more and get more when I can see my faces. The facial expressions give me more to work with."

One time Diane didn't get the eye contact was when she was telling ghost stories to a group of 10,000. "There was a wall of darkness in front of me. The lighting was great for the audience but awful for me. As I told my story the crowd got exceptionally quiet. You could have heard a pin drop. Because I couldn't see their faces, I didn't know if they were engrossed in the story or just respectfully quiet. I learned later that they were spellbound by my storytelling. I really wish I had known because I would have added more to the story and really scared them."

Diane's travel schedule takes her around the country and at times she finds it hard to balance her career with her home life and business paperwork. Recognizing this, she has learned to say no to some jobs. Right now her teenagers are a primary concern and take priority when conflicts arise. For the increasingly overwhelming paperwork, Diane has hired help for the filing and organizing.

To do a good job, Diane says you have to be willing to learn your trade and work up from the bottom. Be willing to pay your dues; you'll be prepared when your time comes. Ask questions. Read. Talk. "Especially with your family, talk a lot and share your heritage in the form of stories. Where TV and videos hamper communication, stories give the strength and backbone to go and be proud of who you are."

The Angle on Chapter 7

*It's no
use making
improvements when you
can't evaluate how well it's going.
The Proof Positive chapter outlines three easy
and effective methods for you to track and visually
measure how something is working...or isn't. At times
we can sniff out lousy conclusions. But even the most
suspicious can be fooled. Why not use a few
tools that take the guesswork
out of finding what really
happened?
RG*

7

PROOF POSITIVE WITH EXPERIMENTAL DESIGNS
Rick Griggs

Your department or work team can only benefit by improving skills at presenting results. Many preventive efforts go unnoticed and great teamwork produces elegant solutions that are never applied to real problems. You can maximize the impact of preventive efforts and solid solutions when you employ basic principles of experimental design in ways that will get everyone to say that's proof positive—this group knows what it's doing.

It's amazing how some people think that the right statistic with the perfect decimal point will support any argument. Others believe the glowing accounts of faith healing, UFO's, and golf scores! Your team's credibility and future existence depend on the substantiated results you achieve.

All of us at one time or another weave a little "white lie" or stretch the information to support our team, our approach or our ideas. The business world should not allow this to go too far. The time has come to use powerful, yet practical tools for documenting the tangible and subtle results of your programs.

When it comes to programs that deal with people's lives and the health of an organization, the slanted information and hidden nuances should be identified and corrected. Your programs cannot afford to suffer from biased and one-sided attacks. Neither can you afford to miss out on the chance to clearly demonstrate the positive effects your services yield. This section will discuss six basic concepts used by researchers when they need to pinpoint the true results of any program. Some may sound a bit academic but bear with me. There is good reason to understand them.

Next, we will discuss tracking or graphing results and getting the exposure your program needs to remain well respected (not to mention well-funded!). You will also learn about three easy-to-use experimental designs that are valuable in showing cause-and-effect relationships.

I suggest you study the six concepts and the three experimental designs so that you understand them thoroughly. When you do this you will be prepared to put them into your own words when explaining them to others in the organization. There's nothing worse than getting all excited about new ideas only to find that others think it's arrogant mumbo-jumbo. Your task is to base your findings on sound thinking and execution, and then to speak the language of the organization when describing your fantastic results.

WHERE'S THE "BIG DIPPER?"

Trying to show the benefits of health, recreation, quality, substance abuse, and other "people" programs without using accurate terms is like describing the Big Dipper through a stained-glass window. Let's stop using clichés like "fit employees make better employees" or "health/fitness programs directly affect the bottom line." They are true but they lack the precise accuracy that top executives demand.

The six terms to know include: <u>independent</u> variable, <u>dependent</u> variable, <u>baseline</u> data, <u>intervention</u> (treatment) data, <u>reliability</u>, and generalization. Two other terms familiar to most are follow-up and maintenance. Although getting immediate follow-up and long-term maintenance are critical, this section of the chapter walks you through the up-front details of documenting the tangible results of your program.

6 EASY DEFINITIONS

Independent Variable—The factor we manipulate to see if it has an effect. This is tested by first isolating this variable and then watching to see how it affects what we are trying to change or observe. Your program may include work restructure, counseling, benchmarking, skills training, focus groups, child care, TQM groups or customer service teams. Any, or all can be considered the independent variable because they are used to see if there are changes in other things you are monitoring and charting.

Dependent Variable—The end result of an experiment. Examples include the smile or frown on your kid's face after trying a new cereal or the raise or pink slip after trying a creative new idea. The dependent variable is the "effect" part of the "cause-effect" relationship. In many corporate programs this factor would be rates of absenteeism, turnover, and productivity. Also included would be the usual reductions in defects, complaints, and general customer/client loss.

Baseline Data—Used as an indication of normal performance before anything is changed. In other words, previous defects, customer service levels or other types of performance, would be used as baseline data. This data is compared with whatever happens after the program is in place. An example would be six months of enrollment records just before a tuition reimbursement plan was overhauled. This baseline phase is considered the benchmark and must always be included to show a change in any behavior pattern.

Intervention (Treatment) Data—Refers to performance while the program or independent variable is in place. Remember that in experiments we manipulate the independent variable to see how it will affect the dependent variable. Both the baseline and treatment data are measures of the dependent variable. It's really not complicated; it just means measuring pulse rates, customer responses, absenteeism or work performance before and during your intervention program. This phase should be watched carefully to be sure nothing gets in the way to muddy the waters. An example is when a bailiff makes comments during a trial that interfere with the jury's deliberations. This is called "confounding" when it occurs during that important intervention phase of a project or an experiment.

Reliability—Can mean the degree to which your results are consistent as time goes on or whether the improvements noticed by one person would also be noticed by others. All good experiments must be repeatable. This replication of results is what makes or breaks good research. You'll remember the unsuccessful attempts to replicate the "cold fusion" claims make by a few researchers. All things being equal, the same training, quality or productivity programs should produce consistent benefits (or problems) from year to year, department to department, and company to company. Accounts of super-healthy employees, sky-high productivity, and ear-to-ear smiles, must be seen by more than one person if your program is to get its share of the credit!

Generalization—Can be complex but it simply means that skills learned in one area can be used in other areas. This applies to fears as well. After a child gets stung by a bee any flying insect can bring tears. A good Total Quality program teaches discipline, patience, consistency, measurement, and correction. All of these skills generalize into other valuable areas of organizational life. It's no wonder those who maintain health, stress, and family programs, generalize many of the same valuable skills and principles into the work setting.

Behavioral researchers have found that after people improve one area of their lives, like their appearance, their speech or their personal wellness, they tend to continue improving other facets as well. When an employee learns the skills to overcome a specific interpersonal problem, the same skills tend to generalize to other issues.

Your program is the independent variable that you claim will benefit individual employees and the organization in general . Now you've got to prove it! The dependent variable is your "proof positive" that these programs work. You will, of course, want to speak everyday language to describe your confidence in the program, but basing your arguments on sound experimental guidelines will make you much more credible. By building your program around these six concepts you can quickly identify parts that don't fit in or just aren't carrying their load. An early warning system like this makes good sense and sure helps build flexible teams.

AN EASY EXAMPLE

Let's suppose a large firm notices an employee turnover problem. A middle manager thinks it's all due to the lack of nearby child care facilities.

The manager retains a licensed operator and opens a facility within walking distance (independent variable). Top management is sold on the idea that it will decrease turnover (dependent variable). The manager make a graph of the turnover rate over the past 18 months (retroactive baseline data).

Reliability is tested by having two different departments collect the turnover information. It could also be demonstrated by repeating the experiment in another division.

Finally, the manager is promoted because not only was the child care fantastically successful in decreasing turnover, it also improved attendance, morale, and recruitment referrals (generalization)!

TRACKING AND GRAPHING

By far, the essential element in documenting the results of any program is to clearly track before and after performance.

You want a quick visual impact. Your baseline data should be tracked for a period of weeks, months or even years. Sometimes you can't afford to wait for weeks or months before starting a program. A "retroactive baseline" solves this problem. This is where you go into records that have already been collected to get your starting point. It may be medical records, work productivity, attendance or other performance measures. You need to be sure these past records are accurate and believable.

Untrusted data are just as bad as lousy data. Many sharp administrators and team leaders will add a short baseline of their own just to be sure the information reflects the current situation.

Charts and graphs should be labeled with a title, a horizontal label and a vertical label. The horizontal line or axis goes across the bottom and is usually in days, weeks or months. A vertical label or axis, usually percentages of productivity, customer responses, attendance, etc. is on the left side of the page.

Your purpose in making line graphs, bar graphs or even fancy scattergrams is only to get a pure snapshot of reality. To this end, it's best to have someone not overly interested in the outcome available to collect and chart the data. Many computer programs are excellent in that they take raw data and produce your graphs or pie-chart at the touch of a key. Avoid getting too fancy!

EXPOSING YOURSELF

Every good program needs exposure. Just like products, businesses and inventions, many goods ones die due to lack of publicity and exposure. A good counseling, benefits or wellness program will no doubt help employees and the organization. You jeopardize the long-term future of the program if you neglect to make the successes known. If it works, then put your reputation on the line to say so.

Excellent methods of publicity include memos, awards, news releases, electronic mail, and company newsletters. When an individual makes personal progress, someone should write a brief note to their boss. By mentioning this kind of progress you will see more of it and get more support for it. Motivational experts say that anything that gets attention will be repeated.

3 EXPERIMENTAL DESIGNS

PRE- & POST-TEST DESIGN- This is the classic "before and after" snapshot to see if there is change. To use this in your programs you would develop a before and after measure for performance. It could be a 10 question quiz, a step test, body fat percentages, customer responses or a 30 question multiple choice exam. You would then administer the test at the beginning of the program and an identical or similar one at the end. Many people prefer to give different versions of the same quiz or test so the answers cannot be memorized. The difference in scores, or the "delta," is considered to be the result of the program.

A-B-A-B REVERSAL DESIGN- This is another way to show that your program actually "caused" an effect to occur. The A portion can be considered the baseline, and the B is the treatment or intervention. You would start with a baseline measure of performance and then go into the program. Normally, you will see a difference in performance as you go from the first A phase into the first B phase. At this point there may be questions as to what really caused the change. A simple A-B design leaves too many possibilities or other reasons for the change. By returning to the A or baseline phase you can reverse the progress made by your program.

Hold on! Before you scream bloody murder about reversing good progress just to show someone, let me explain. Some programs can afford to remove the intervention and return to the baseline phase in order to remove all doubt. This "reversal" back to the A phase is just to show how much of an effect the program really has. You would then finish with the second B phase. This could be done with areas such as absenteeism, course enrollment, customer opinions, where the information is vital but the reversal would not do much damage. You can always reinstate the program to everyone's applause. You would never use the A-B-A-B Reversal design with programs dealing with alcoholism, depression or critical performance areas.

MULTIPLE BASELINE DESIGN- Here is what you've been waiting for. This method of documentation eliminates the need for reversing good progress. You would start by selecting three problems, customer concerns or quality issues. All you do is sequentially administer treatment (your program) at separate times to all three.

After a baseline has been established for all three, you start the program on one. While one is getting the program the others are simply being monitored. Their baselines are being extended. After a week or two, you start the program on the second problem. Now problems one and two are getting the "treatment" while number three is still in the baseline phase. Later you add number three to those getting the program.

Assuming the program is working, you will have created a powerful demonstration of its benefits. The multiple baseline design takes a little more effort and time but the results are visual and dynamically convincing. It can be easily used with different people, separate departments or various projects.

Never fool yourself. Use these six concepts and three experimental designs to document the concrete benefits of your programs. If they're not working, shouldn't you be the first to know? And if they are, these tools will help you spread the news in a meaningful way.

POINTS TO REMEMBER/THINGS TO DO

1. Limit your measurement activities to truly important things.
2. The best systems are open, honest, and flexible.
3. Remember, in a study, only change the "independent variable," so you'll know if it worked.
4. Focus on "generalization" to expand positive changes and results.
5. Use the Pre-Post design for easy to track issues.
6. Use the A-B-A-B Reversal design for better proof of results.
7. Try the Multiple Baseline design to test a great solution in different departments or on different problems.
8. Avoid "Tantalus" by getting the facts early. Above all, don't be the last to know.

Mission & Success Factors Sample

We are creating a new industry based on Balanced Achievement. By combining the best of the training and motivation fields, we offer consulting/training, products, and publications that teach individuals and groups how to reach goals. The result is sustained accomplishment by well-rounded professionals. Like the elements of a masterpiece, we integrate the Factors of Achievement. We run our business with the highest respect and concern for our employees, our clients, and our associates.

COMPANY SUCCESS FACTORS

1. Research and develop training, products, and publications that teach achievement.

2. Maintain strategic alliances with outside resource experts for support of the mission.

3. Market services to the correct people who decide, purchase, and apply them to solutions.

4. Develop and publicize an accurate and exciting company identity.

5. Build favorable exposure and relations with the infrastructure of our markets, including trade/business press, distributors, publishers, and human resource professionals.

6. Attract, retain, and richly reward personnel who are outstanding in the areas of Performance, Initiative, and Loyalty.

7. Maintain fair levels of profitability in all divisions while remaining true to our mission.

8. Adhere to a strategy of diversification to ensure cash flow, maintain a strong balance sheet, and enhance economies of scale among all divisions in ads, publicity, and cross-over opportunities.

9. Demonstrate complete customer satisfaction by making nothing more important than meeting the needs of our clients.

10. Maintain integrity and credibility by respecting and protecting the rights and esteem of our staff, our associates, and our clients.

Mission & Success Factors Worksheet

AGENCY/ORGANIZATIONAL MISSION:

_____
_____
_____

DEPARTMENT/GROUP MISSION:

_____
_____
_____

SUCCESS FACTORS:

1._____

2._____

3._____

4._____

5._____

6._____

7._____

8._____

9._____

10._____

A. The mission should be explored, updated, and discussed. Allow time for group comments and individual assimilation.

B. The department mission or vision should carve out the portion of the overall mission that relates to it.

C. All department activities and responsibilities should be reflected in at least one of the success factors.

(Permission granted to copy this form after purchase of book)

Angle View 17
SAVE THE COWBOYS
Lynn - Rodeo bullfighter/clown

"My job is to protect the cowboy bull rider. I distract the bull away from the cowboy so he won't get hurt. If the bull rider was to hit the ground, I must step in between the bull and the cowboy and if necessary jump on the bull's head and 'take a hooking' so the cowboy won't have to. That's my job."

Meet Lynn—three time world champion professional rodeo bullfighter/clown. Don't let the clown costume trick you into thinking his is an easy job. Entertaining the crowd is just a small part of his work. A bullfighter must be able to think and move quickly. He must be smart and have a thorough understanding of a bull's strengths and limitations. He must be able to get "in sync" with an animal ten to twelve times his own weight. Lynn's job is demanding, dangerous and life threatening. He does it with pride. He does it because he loves it. He is acknowledged as one of the best. What motivates Lynn? What are his quality standards?

"It's a great feeling to be able to control a 2,000 pound animal and make him come in the direction that I choose. I know bulls are distracted by moving targets. I make myself that target to protect the downed cowboy. It's intense. It's hard. There's nothing like getting right next to an animal that big when you know he's trying to harm you, yet with one or two steps you can force him to whiz right past you. That's power. That's intensity!"

Lynn, a former bull rider whose home is in South Dakota, has kept up that intensity for almost 10 years. The job has taken its toll; he's had two serious "hookings"—one to the ribs, and another to the face which required 42 stitches and plastic surgery. But at 30, he feels he has a good 10 years to go.

A good quality day for Lynn is a day no cowboy gets hurt. On those days he leaves the bullfighter/rodeo clown part of him in the arena and can leave with a clear conscience. If a cowboy gets hurt, it's a different scenario. "If somebody gets hurt because I wasn't there at the right time," said Lynn, "I won't mentally leave the arena. I won't speak to anyone. I'll go back to my hotel and rehearse the incident in my mind over and over again. I'll figure out what went wrong, where I should have been, and how I can make sure that it

127

doesn't ever happen again. Only after I've concluded that mental evaluation, can I give it up. I take cowboys' injuries very personally. If a cowboy gets hurt, I didn't do my job well."

The same concern for the well being of the cowboy extends to the animals. Once during a rodeo, a bucking bull broke his leg during a ride. Lynn yelled for the cowboy to jump off, but the bull, in a frenzy, kept bucking. To calm the animal and get him out of his spin, Lynn slapped him in the face. The action worked, but in the process, Lynn got horned in the ribs. The calm bull walked out of the arena and was shot. Lynn went to the hospital. Ironically, Lynn saved the bull from further harming himself even though Lynn knew the bull would be shot.

"I hate to see animals get hurt; I hate to see anybody get hurt. But in this business it happens. It's dangerous. But the animals in the circuit are well taken care of. Many are very valuable and are actually better treated than many family pets. They are valued at between $3,000 and $5,000."

The life of a rodeo bullfighter is one of travel, hotels and suitcases. There is a tremendous camaraderie among the cowboys, but the life is certainly different from most. Lynn's definition of balance reflects that lifestyle. "For me, balance means happiness. If I'm happy I'm balanced. I see a lot of death. I have to learn to deal with it. I didn't ask to come here and I'm not going to ask to leave - that's balance."

When asked about how he stays happy in such a dangerous occupation, he laughed. "I do a lot of laughing," Lynn commented, "and I keep a positive attitude. A positive attitude is very important. I wake up. I look in the mirror. I look great! I feel great! I am great!

Angle View 18
1000 HEAVENLY VOICES
Marge - Professional Whistler

Marge has been described as having the ability to create "the quiet when you listen to thousands of heavenly voices of angels speaking through one instrument." Her instrument is her voice. Her skill is artistic whistling.

Marge is the only professional artistic whistler in the country and owns the right to the only artistic whistling school anywhere. Her definition of artistic whistling is "the art of putting bird songs into linguistic form within the timing of music so that it is both pleasing to the ear and healing to the soul." She continued, "Like an Olympic ice skater twirling and spinning to the music or a painter conveying his or her feelings on canvas, I put feelings in sound, I am a musician."

Whistling became a part of Marge's life as early as the age of 3. And, as she puts it, she's somewhere between 40 and 80 so she's been whistling for a long time. For nine years she studied at the Agnes Stuart School of Whistling; the rights to which she now owns and calls the California School of Artistic Whistling. For the past twelve years she has performed as a full time professional whistler and teacher who has taught between 55 and 60 aspiring artistic whistlers. Her work in 1990 logged her over 33,000 miles whistling around the country.

How can you tell quality in an artistic whistler? "Properly done artistic whistling is never shrill or abrasive," said Marge. "It is a very pure sound with round tones - very mellow. There's never too much vibrato; it's not too tight and never squeaky." Often, Marge says people can't stand to hear a whistler for more than a half-minute because many whistlers have abrasive tones. You can't teach a person to whistle. They either have it or they don't. If they have the ability to whistle, I can teach them the special qualities of artistic whistling. But only those with true intrinsic talent are going to be really good. I'm very lucky, I have a God given talent. I also have true pitch. I'm so unique; nobody does what I do."

Marge's talents have been appreciated in some very unusual ways. Studies at several large universities have proven that plants have cells that respond to sound. When the cells are stimulated with the

129

appropriate sounds, they are 700 times more receptive to organic plant nutrients sprayed on to encourage growth than when there is no sound. The special sounds are, not surprisingly, bird songs. Did you think birds sang only for personal pleasure? Maybe to spread the joy of morning wake-up to sleepy risers? Apparently all things have a purpose and they too have a job to do! ...Oops...back to the story...A large major plant nutrient company commissioned Marge to record her voice whistling bird songs with musical accompaniment (minus percussion—plant cells don't like that!). That record is now played throughout the fields of the plant nutrient company at feeding time to help with their research on plant growth.

Her notoriety goes well beyond her work stimulating plant growth. Marge has four albums and is working on a fifth. She has been interviewed and sang on CNN and was even a guest on "What's My Line?" Marge has whistled for groups as large as 160,000 and as small as one. In fact, some of her most memorable performances have been one-on-one and small group whistling for groups such as children, seniors and the deaf. Deaf people cannot hear the frequency of voices but they can hear the frequency of whistling; often that is the only music they can hear. Many a deaf person has expressed personal delight at Marge's performances - many were brought to tears from hearing their first "music" ever.

Marge credits part of her success with having a balanced life including a good family, many friends and the opportunity to do what she loves with a passion. For years she worked as a dental hygienist before retiring. Sometimes a goal has to be put off until the proper time, but as Marge knew, the time would come. She said, "I decided when I quit my J-O-B I would dedicate my life to making people happy. You see, everybody understands what I'm doing because they don't have to understand the words. This is a wonderful profession. I thrill people. I make people happy. I make people feel better. I love what I do."

Her love is obvious to the people who hear her because she follows her own advice: "Be sincerely cordial with people. Speak and act as if it were a genuine pleasure to perform the service or do the job. If you don't want to do something, get out, do something else. Life's too short."

Angle View 19
"I RIDE THE BULLS"
Bryan - Professional Bull Rider

Bryan is an experienced athlete and competitor who's "gone done the road." That's the expression cowboys use for traveling the rodeo circuit. At age 26, Bryan is one of a small number of ethnic cowboys on the pro rodeo circuit. He is also a champion with an impressive list of credentials. Bryan was a district champion bull rider in high school and was number 11 in world standings at the end of 1988. In that same year he was the Sierra Pro Rodeo Circuit bull riding champion. Also in 1988 he reached his highest national ranking, number three, just before an injury sidelined him for months.

Bryan believes in himself and has a mindset that he feels will fuel his rise to the top in his field, Says Bryan, "I ride bulls and I'm among the elite in my field. I'm betting on my ability, my mental preparation and how many bulls I've ridden. It's a gamble, but it's fun. Going down the road, I've seen more country and met more people than the average American. Even with all the injuries I wouldn't give it back."

A quality ride for Bryan has two components, timing and style. The goal is clear, 'beat the bull' as the animal angrily bucks and spins to 'beat the cowboy.' "It's me against the bull," said Bryan. "Before I worry about winning, I have to beat the bull; I have to make those eight seconds. After that, I worry how the judges score me."

Staying in shape also has two components. Bryan, who has suffered several serious injuries, has a rigorous daily physical regimen which includes weight training, running and other aerobic exercises. Equally important is his mental training, which he describes as critical to success. There's a certain 'psych' that's necessary. "Bull riding is self conscious. You can't pump yourself up just before you get on - it comes from years of experience - you get on and let it flow." Part of Bryan's mental training involves purposeful mental imagery. Bryan explained, "Getting on practice bulls is good, but I can't do that every day. I do it in my mind. I continually imagine myself riding, mentally, and having a good score. Only after the mental practice can I do it physically. My imagining myself riding bulls is just about as good as me getting on."

Another mental toughening technique Bryan uses is to listen to goal setting tapes. He says the tapes have nothing directly to do with bull riding, but talk about goals and how to successfully attain them. "The tapes," he said, "are not instant pump-ups but a look at other people's accomplishments and challenges or ruts they've overcome." Bryan feels these have been a tremendous help to him. They can also be helpful in dealing with slumps.

"You have slumps. You're going to get bumped off a lot of bulls— that's the nature of the profession. People tell you you're in a slump, you start thinking you're in a slump, and then you really will be in a slump. It's not all going to be easy. Some times are going to be hard. But you have to have the courage to stay with it.

Bryan has the courage. He has stayed with the sport for 12 years; 6 as a professional. His outlook on the dangerous aspects are matter-of-fact. Passion is his guide. "I've had friends get killed riding bulls. That's the saddest part of the job. It's even sadder when people know what I do and come up to me and say, "You need to start looking for a different profession." I'll shoot right back telling them that people die in car accidents every year, so your telling me to quit bull riding is the same as me telling you to stop driving. If it's your time to go, you're going to go. If you're going to get injured, you're going to get injured. If anything was going to stop me it would have been in my rookie year when I broke my femur. I had to sit out for 15 months with a metal rod in my leg. I couldn't get on anything. That didn't stop me."

All told, Bryan wears his cowboy status proudly. Characteristically dressed in a white hat and blue jeans, his personality mirrors his motto, "Tough times never last, tough people do." Bryan practices what he preaches when he says, "No matter what you do—bull rider, lawyer, street sweeper—be the best at whatever you do. If you're going to do it, be the best. You've got to believe in yourself all the time. You can't want anything. You've got to go get it."

The Angle on Chapter 8

*This part
is for those with a
basic statistical background
who want to delve a bit deeper
into the quantifiable aspects of quality.
Gregory Swartz writes about "crispy critters"
and statistical methods. These tools are for
the professional and the aficionado who
want expanded knowledge and
skills to go along with the
other "angles" presented
in this book.
RG*

8

TOTAL QUALITY & CONTINUOUS IMPROVEMENT
Gregory R. Swartz

The purpose of this chapter will be to show how products and their processes can be vastly improved via the use of continuous improvement tools. Presented up front, will be an example of two problem solving tools in action. This is followed by a powerful, but often overlooked tool called Pareto Analysis. Process Capability and Six Sigma are defined with an industrial example. A discussion of variation is included to acquaint you with some of the basics.

The chapter deals a strategic card in your Quality Process tool kit for "Continuous Improvement." Even though people have a dreaded fear of "Statistical Analysis," it can be made understandable and is a valuable Quality improvement tool. Statistics are now becoming an essential tool in the decision making process, reflecting the quality improvement efforts in both our products and processes.

This chapter is not a text book on statistics nor is it a complete reference on SPC. However, it does provide a map if you will, to assist in your own decision making process for quality. Simply put, the chapter will guide you through a Continuous Improvement Process and present key points for a successful implementation plan.

Here is an outline of what will be covered in this chapter:

VARIATION AND CONTINUOUS IMPROVEMENT
     A. Natural and Unnatural Causes
     B. Sources of Variation
PROCESS AND IMPROVEMENT
     A. Process Flow Analysis
     B. Brainstorming Procedure
     C. Pareto Analysis
PROCESS CAPABILITY AND SIX SIGMA
     A. What is Process Capability and Six Sigma?
     B. An Industry Example
SPC IMPLEMENTATION
     A. Purpose
     B. SPC Team Concept
     C. Training and Implementation
CONCLUSION

I. <u>VARIATION AND CONTINUOUS IMPROVEMENT</u>

Things really do vary as they do. Variation is a fact in nature as well as in the workplace. Think of the times you arrive at work or get up in the morning. Are you always exactly on time? The definition of variation is directly weighted by the factors that influence it.

Variation, for example, is fundamental to all industries. In agriculture, it is measured in the growth rates of produce yields and hybrids. The confidence in clinical studies is caused by, and based largely upon variance. But, what are the types of variation that exist and what causes things to vary so much?

The reasons can be broken down to two major categories as shown in Table I.

Table I

TWO TYPES OF VARIATION

NORMAL	ABNORMAL
Common Causes	Special Causes
Systematic	Localized
By Chance	Assignable Cause
Stable	Unstable

It stands to reason that one might ask the question: Which types of causes (special or common) of variation might I approach first? Well, to make life simpler (and we'd like that), a more logical path to take would be first to attack the special causes. These are those occurrences in variation that are not necessarily due to chance, but are *assignable and correctable*.

The premise is this: When first charting or characterizing a process, many sporadic types of variation may be discovered. So, the first step to take in variance reduction is to eliminate all assignable or special causes up front, reducing "noise" in the process. Next, go about the business of overall variance reduction. The latter would be our *common cause system*, necessitating both management participation and support.

Listed below in Table II are some of the sources of variation. They are similar to those found in Cause and Effect Diagrams.

Table II

VARIATION SOURCES

People	Methods
Equipment	Environment
Materials	Measurement

The next section will tie these sources of variation into a cause and effect diagram. A process flow analysis is presented first on a service related problem. This will help in showing how a process improvement tool works in a real application.

II. <u>PROCESS AND IMPROVEMENT</u>

The search for continuous improvement is something people have always strived for. But, how does one measure improvement or decide when a particular process or system has, in fact, made a significant improvement—beyond a shadow of a doubt?

Let's first decide upon or come to some agreement as to what processes are. After all, a definition of a process is essential, prior to our attempts to improve it. For example, a firm's main product may be clothing but it also involves the delivery of the articles to customers' residences. For ease in description, we will call this company "Attractive Apparels."

DIAGRAMMING HOW IT FLOWS

A process flow diagram would help us in determining specific process points of interest in the delivery of Attractive Apparels. The simple process diagram below outlines the essential steps in sequence (boxes indicate process steps):

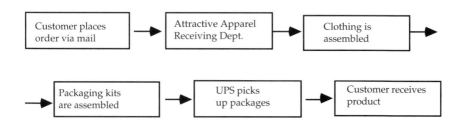

Now that we have a process diagram, the lay person may think, "Well, that's nice, but, how do I go about actually improving this process?" Or another way of stating the question may be: "What improvement is going to have the greatest impact for my customer?"

This is where you, as the investigator, come into the picture. It is now your turn to collaborate with your peers and associates to brainstorm on possible causes of potential problems that the customer is experiencing. Let's say for example, with Attractive Apparels that fit, seems to be the customer's and the company's biggest problem.

Our diagram of the process can be helpful in resolving key issues for this particular problem of customer fit. We can use the same process flow diagram with additional limbs to help in our brainstorming activity. This second diagram now takes a new shape which looks like a fish bone. The procedure for brainstorming a fishbone diagram is simple.

BRAINSTORMING PROCEDURE:

Below is given a typical procedure for identifying, brainstorming and then taking corrective action on a problem. For demonstration purposes, the Attractive Apparel will be presented to show continuous improvement on the process. Let's begin.

A. VERIFY—that you have a distinct problem appropriate for the group brainstorming process. Fishbone Diagrams can be used for a variety of situations or problems. Often, the main problem or item of concern is placed in the right-hand box of the cause and effect diagram. For our example, Customer Fit is placed in the right hand box in our example on the next page.

B. BRAINSTORM ALL POSSIBLE ROOT CAUSES—This is the fun step where you, your peers, and collaborators must think of and write down various causes that can contribute to your problem, e.g., customer's clothing fit. Remember while brainstorming, no cause should be eliminated or judged. Simply write every idea that comes to mind onto one of the appropriate bones of the fishbone diagram.

See the example on the next page:

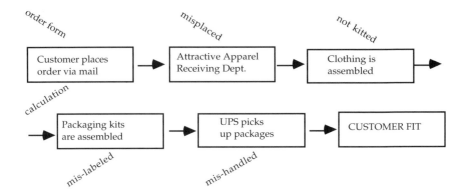

WHAT DO I HAVE?

C. ANALYSIS—Now, after brainstorming all possible causes to a problem, it is suggested to select a limb off the fishbone diagram that seems to have a direct influence on your problem. For instance, Customer Orders may have more items than one of the other boxes. This will not only help determine the root cause(s) of your identified problem, but will also point to where you may need to collect additional data.

YOUR NEXT STEP is to either take corrective action on root causes listed off your fishbone diagram, or you may need to collect additional data. Our next improvement tool will help prioritize these causes.

PARETO ANALYSIS

Pareto Analysis is also known as "The 80-20 effect" where most problems result from just a few causes. The objective of the analysis is to separate the "Vital Few" from the "Trivial Many." The top few causes comprise the majority of lost time, money, and effort in productivity and quality.

The ADVANTAGES are as follows:

- Improving the largest problem decreases the overall defective percentage of product.
- Cost of lost product can easily be determined with the assistance of Pareto Analysis.
- Saves both time and money. Profits are gained from improvement.

MORE ON PARETO
(for Categorical Data)

This procedure requires a check sheet for your data, which lists the potential causes for a specific problem such as the one that follows with customer complaints. Keep in mind that Pareto will assist in resolving the major problem. As an added plus, a cost Pareto analysis is shown to justify the R.O.I. (return on investment) on such an analysis.

A. VERIFY—See that you have already done a Check Sheet prior to making a Pareto Chart. Make sure that the Check Sheet you use for this chart contains categorical data such as defective parts, types of defects or types of supplies, for example.

B. PURPOSE—To organize and show data, such as missing parts or defective items, so that the highest occurring problem can be easily identified and shown in a graph.

The following example of Field Service problems shows the percentage of Customer Complaints.

See diagram on next page.

FIELD SERVICE CUSTOMER COMPLAINTS:

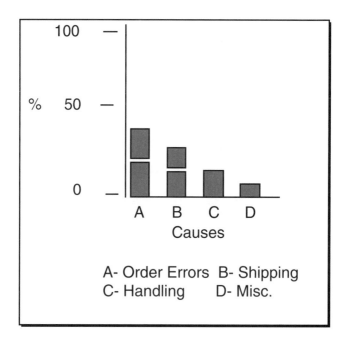

In the figure on the next page, cost data can provide additional insight into deciding which problem should be of most concern in terms of getting your Return On Investment (ROI). Where a secondary cause of failures may not initially seem important, following a cost Pareto analysis, you can come up with some real data showing the potential cost savings to the organization.

See diagram on next page.

COST TO RESPOND TO FIELD SERVICE COMPLAINTS:

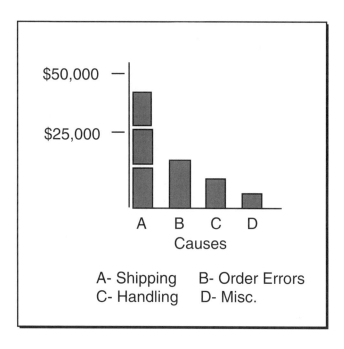

$40,000 Shipping
$15,000 Orders
$10,000 Handling
$ 5,000 Misc.

Upon closer inspection of the types of complaints, even though order entry errors occurred most often, shipping errors were the most costly. So we would focus our corrective action on shipping types of errors in this case. After you have done a Pareto analysis, ask yourself the following question:

INTERPRETING THE PARETO

C. ANALYSIS—By looking at your Pareto Chart, you can identify your most frequent or most costly items. This is the 80-20 concept presented earlier, where a majority of your problems result from just one or two primary causes. These causes are usually represented by the first two bars in your Pareto chart.

D. YOUR NEXT STEP—is to take corrective action on the vital few or primary causes identified on your Pareto chart—in our example, shipping—since it was the most costly defect. The next step could be to use another Fishbone diagram to brainstorm the possible causes. In this example, shipping errors would be a focal point since they were the most costly.

III. <u>PROCESS CAPABILITY AND SIX SIGMA</u>

Process Capability tells the problem solver whether or not his/her process is truly capable of meeting the customer's requirement or specification. This specification could also be drawn from an internal customer as well. This would be the next step in a process flow. If the distribution width is outside the specification width, then the process is not capable and most likely, a defective product is made. The Capability Index (Cp or Cpk) is one means of proving if the process is capable or not. This may get confusing, but here goes.

The formulas for the Indices show that a process under statistical control, which exhibits a normal distribution, will indicate that 99.73% of the output will fall with plus or minus three (3) standard deviations of the mean of the distribution. The common base for computing the various indices is the six (6) standard deviation (6 sigma) width. If all of this sounds complicated, bear with me. It's very useful and it gets a bit easier as we go along.

An Industry Example

Process Control and Process Capability are two "Angles" or ways of helping us understand and better define our processes. This would hold true for practically any product or process-related industry. Process Control deals with the inherent natural, or sometimes unnatural, variation in our processes. Process Capability on the other hand, is a concept even more closely related to the actual quality of our products. Let's take a brief look at the following example:

A potato chip factory, "Crispy Critters" is very interested in producing crisp potato chips for its customer base. This implies certain quality characteristics, say freshness, crunchiness, and other delectable descriptors for a high quality potato chip. Since I'm a potato manufacturer (for the example), I happen to be very interested in my customer's satisfaction and repeatability of purchases.

From our previous brainstorming tool on how to make improvements, we learned that diagramming and analyzing the root causes of a major customer problem will often induce an improved customer rapport. Say for instance, "Crispy Critters" has brainstormed, and discovered that staleness is a problem in outlying distribution centers It was determined that a minimum specification of humidity be closely monitored and controlled.

In lay person's terms, "Crispy Critters" had humidity under some expected normal occurrence without too much variation. An inquisitive investigator, with a somewhat different "angle" on quality—*process capability* —wanted to see if both factories had humidity well below the required specification, for example, humidity $\leq 20\%$.

PROCEDURE

Let's take a look at how the investigator did it. First of all, he needed separate humidity samples from each of the "Crispy Critters" factory sites. He came up with the following results over a thirty day period.

Factory One	**Factory Two**
Avg. Humidity	Avg. Humidity
$\bar{\chi} = 16\%$	$\bar{\chi} = 17\%$
Standard Deviation	Standard Deviation
$\acute{o} = 2.0\%$	$\acute{o} = .5\%$

At first glance, one might think that Factory #2 is setting a poor example, since their average humidity of 17% is higher than Factory #1. However, the average is not all that important, for the Standard Deviation ($\acute{o}$, as a measure of variation) will in fact contribute in determining which factory is well within the specification, and conversely which factory is not. Our objective will be to resolve which factory has the highest overall humidity, in order to determine the root cause of the stale chips.

Capability Index (Cpk) defined

Random samples of humidity are collected. Any biased or spurious data are minimized, so that results are not confounded (ruined or tainted). Remember, in this particular case of high humidity, we are really only concerned with an Upper Specification (US), that is, humidity should not exceed 20%. The detailed procedure for Factory #1 is listed below:

Factory #1 Cpk is equal to the following:

Avg. Humidity $\bar{\chi}$ = 16%

US - Average/3ó = $\underline{20\text{-}16}$ = .667   Standard Deviation, ó = 2.0%
$\qquad\qquad\qquad\quad$ 3 x 2.0

Cpk is the relative index or Capability index of our process. If this number is greater than one, our process is truly capable of meeting the specification. In our Factory #1 example, it is not capable, since our Cpk is less than one.
Remember: A Cpk > 1 indicates that the process is capable.

Now, let's perform the same test for Factory #2, which we assumed was worse because of higher humidity at 17%.

Factory #2 Cpk is equal to the following:

Avg. Humidity $\bar{\chi}$= 17%

US - Average / 3ó = $\underline{20\text{-}17}$ = 2.00   Standard Deviation, ó = 0.5%
$\qquad\qquad\qquad\quad$ 3 x 0.5

WHAT DO YOU THINK?

Upon first glance at the data, one might suspect Factory #2 as having the worst humidity. However, Factory #2 indeed had less variability with a Standard Deviation of only .5%. Factory #2 also had a Cpk value of 2.00 indicating that its process was very capable! In fact, even though Factory #1 had the lower average humidity, it was less capable of meeting the humidity specification, because its variability was significantly higher at 2%, and a disappointing Cpk value of only .667. The corrective action in this case would be to focus on Factory #1 in order to reduce its high variability in humidity.

Finally, the Standard Deviation, (ó) can give us a lot of information about the variation of our products and critical processes. To a large extent, it will determine the capability of the process, and help us in our improvement efforts. Now for some other thoughts on SPC or Statistical Process Control Implementation. Just remember, that nothing is set in concrete. Ultimately your Continuous Improvement Program will need some personal customization. Implementation guidelines and keys are just ahead to assist in your program.

IV. SPC IMPLEMENTATION

Purpose of the Implementation Program

The main purpose of the implementation program is to provide operations with adequate tools, training, and resources to implement Statistical Process Control (SPC) into key areas of the manufacturing process. One of the primary vehicles to accomplish this task is the development of core groups called SPC Teams. This, along with the proper training and implementation, will collectively create an atmosphere of learning and success in your production areas. The components of SPC teams, training, and implementation are presented as follows:

SPC TEAM CONCEPT

It is suggested that the SPC Team Concept begins with assigning manufacturing personnel to work on key projects within selected areas. Since these are often the first SPC Projects within manufacturing, these projects may or may not be targeted at critical process steps, for example, ones with low yield or high quality costs, such as scrap and rework. Rather, they should be selected to provide a clear demonstration of the effectiveness of SPC, develop organizational commitment, and train key employees in the process. An in-house or external resource consultant should assist the teams in selecting which areas would be most appropriate for introducing

SPC, but because of the ownership issue discussed previously, final project selection is left to the teams.

The SPC Team consists of groups of individuals selected from each key production area. For example, in semiconductor manufacturing, typical areas could be Assembly, Mask Shop, Diffusion, Photo, and Test. Each team will be chartered to plan and implement Statistical Process Control at a single key step within the process. They are to demonstrate the effectiveness of SPC in reducing the amount of scrap and rework, thereby enhancing quality, yield, and productivity. Additionally, the establishment of the core groups will set the precedent for future SPC projects. The SPC teams consist of four to six members selected from the previously mentioned manufacturing areas. An example of an ideal configuration for the groups is to have a team consisting of the following:

1. Operations Supervisor
2. All Shift Supervisors
3. Engineering Supervisor responsible for area
4. Maintenance Supervisor

There are three main reasons for establishing SPC Teams. They are listed below:

1. To Organize the work structure for proper implementation of SPC and to establish a positive attitude, understanding, and appreciation of the value of this program.

2. To Demonstrate SPC success stories to the organization and the value of SPC as a tool in manufacturing and production areas.

3. To Provide data, experience, and context for an SPC Manual for Operators, so that the knowledge gained will be easily transferred to the shop floor.

TRAINING THE TEAM

The purpose of team training is to educate personnel in the application of various statistical techniques within their SPC Teams. Naturally, for proper implementation of SPC techniques, training in the appropriate tools is essential. So important is this phase of the program, that classes should be mandatory for all SPC Team members. Two sections of training should be delivered during the Implementation program. They are described briefly as follows:

1. *Applied Data Analysis/SPC/Equipment Organization* - The portion instructs engineers in the modern statistical techniques for quickly identifying and correcting problems uncovered with control charts. These techniques, including the so-called "Taguchi Methods," have proven to be very useful for troubleshooting equipment and process problems. In order to achieve a high level of control, team members, especially engineers, will need to engage in process characterization and/or troubleshooting techniques. Statistically designed experiments demonstrate sources of process variation and out-of-control conditions. Prior to training the SPC Teams in the methods, a one-week course in SPC Troubleshooting and Equipment Optimization is useful for sustaining engineers, particularly engineering SPC Team members and their supervisors.

2. *Statistical Process Control* - This part of the implementation program also focuses on the SPC Team approach to solving problems. In this two-day section of the program, basic statistical techniques are presented in such a way as to encourage their direct application to the production process. Team members are exposed to the basic principles of Pareto Diagrams and Ishikawa's Cause and Effect Diagrams.

Following this, an overview of the fundamentals of descriptive statistics, and process capability studies are discussed. The second day of training in SPC focuses on Statistical Process Control Charts, and their interpretation. The latter is coupled with the integration of the SPC Teams' projects and how they are using the tools presented thus far.

This type of program can also serve as a spring-board from which the SPC Teams will identify the target area(s) of concern and delegate the responsibilities of their program. In other words, these activities will set a precedent for future meetings and pave the way for a successful SPC program.

3. *Operations Training Implementation* - SPC implementations generally do not require computer systems for on-going control charts. However, a successful, highly profitable implementation of SPC will demonstrate that SPC is essential to the competitive manufacturer. This in turn, often prompts the future need for

statistical software and computer systems to better automate your processes.

A smart reason for having SPC training up front, is to have personnel understand the application of statistical tools before taking on the next step of applying them in an automated environment. Because implementation is heavily focused on the SPC Teams and their projects, the specifics of the SPC projects are described below.

Implementation entails teams choosing a target process step within its area for application of SPC methods and for the purpose of continued SPC monitoring. The selection of projects ultimately rests with each team in making their own decision. The teams can consider the following:

- opportunities for improvements of high value and visibility
- ability to complete the project on schedule
- impact on production
- availability of data
- project visibility
- types of data

In order to gain a thorough understanding of the selected process steps, SPC project teams need to collect data on the current process. It is also necessary to collect historical and supplementary data during the study period. Most of this needs to be collected periodically, on a lot-by-lot (or batch) basis to statistically characterize production variability.

During this data gathering phase, the team will establish the historical quality of the process, and the capability of the process as it is currently configured. Team members from the manufacturing area are responsible for preparing data collection forms and assuring that they are consistently used across all shifts. Data collection from experiments will be the responsibility of team members from engineering. Data involving machine maintenance of calibration will be gathered by the team member whose normal responsibilities are in those areas.

Most of the analysis of the data is done by team members using the SPC methods taught in the preliminary training. Trainers, engineers and statisticians should assist in this effort and provide other analysis where it is required.

SPC SUCCESS STORIES WITH RESULTS!

Finally, team members should investigate ways to improve quality of the targeted process, and test their ideas with respect to the data. Based on their findings, they will prepare charts for future monitoring and submit reports or success stories containing the findings and recommendations of the team. This will document the improvements they have made in areas such as, yield improvement, variability reduction, cycle time, contamination or breakage. At the end of this project, they can present their report in a management review meeting.

CONCLUSION

The purpose of any Continuous Process Improvement strategy is to investigate, monitor, and naturally improve the quality of goods and services. To this end, the tools presented in this chapter are just a few of the methods and procedures instrumental in the improvement of quality. They are by no means a panacea to all problems, but rather, an integral part of Continuous Process Improvement.

Keep in mind that even the most basic problem solving tools can provide organizations with a good foundation for process improvement. With any Quality Improvement Program such as SPC, it helps to define the problem prior to any attempt to solve it. Hot-House, slogan generating, quality schemes only provide lip service, and rarely get at the root causes of problems.

Hopefully, this chapter has provided you with helpful suggestions for Statistical Process Control implementation using some of the process improvement tools. It is only a guideline for your Continuous Improvement effort. The hope, however, is to provide you with some keys to assist in your own decision making process for quality improvement. Often these efforts result in real cost savings to the company, and a demonstrated return on the investment. As Philip Crosby has emphatically stated, "Quality is Free." It only costs you if you don't have it.

POINTS TO REMEMBER/THINGS TO DO

1. Do perform process capability studies both before and after SPC implementation.
2. Remember, basic problem solving tools, such as Pareto analysis can be just as powerful as more sophisticated techniques.
3. Do monitor critical processes with Statistical Process Control.
4. Establish SPC teams for "Continuous Process Improvement."
5. Remember to plan out a strategy for successful implementation.
6. Perform both pre and post Pareto charts for comparative purposes.
7. Do gather data from your customers (both internal and external). Skipping this part would be classic "Tantalus."
8. Finally, don't forget to reduce variation for process improvement.

Department Goals Inventory

Circle = Past Goals Square = Present Goals NA = Not Applicable

GROUP GOALS		PERCENT (%) COMPLETED									
Overall Quality	0	10	20	30	40	50	60	70	80	90	100
Project ____ Quality	0	10	20	30	40	50	60	70	80	90	100
Project ____ Quality	0	10	20	30	40	50	60	70	80	90	100
Project ____ Quality	0	10	20	30	40	50	60	70	80	90	100
Communication	0	10	20	30	40	50	60	70	80	90	100
Team Relations	0	10	20	30	40	50	60	70	80	90	100
Customer Relations	0	10	20	30	40	50	60	70	80	90	100
Attendance Goals	0	10	20	30	40	50	60	70	80	90	100
Turnover Goals	0	10	20	30	40	50	60	70	80	90	100
Financial Goals	0	10	20	30	40	50	60	70	80	90	100

ADD SOME OF YOUR OWN:

_____	0	10	20	30	40	50	60	70	80	90	100
_____	0	10	20	30	40	50	60	70	80	90	100

YOUR RESULTS!

A. Use one color to connect the circles to see your past trend of accomplishment.

B. With a different color, connect the squares to see how your group is currently progressing.

(Permission granted to copy this form after purchase of book)

Angle View 20
23 QUARTS OF "JALAPEÑO" ICE CREAM?
John - Ice Cream Taster

Without a doubt ice cream is America's number one dessert. You'd find the same statistic in many other countries. Its creamy, smooth, flavorful consistency is enjoyed by 80% of American consumers. Each year we enjoy an average of 23 quarts of ice cream per person! You probably have never heard a young child say he or she wanted to grow up to be an ice cream taster. An ice cream taster? Is that really a profession? Absolutely! And only a few, like the rich cream the desert embodies, rise to the top. One who has risen to that enviable position, is John. He is the flavor developer and official taste tester for a large national premium ice cream company. Although he admits it is a fun profession, ice cream tasting is a serious business—his taste buds are insured for a cool million bucks!

John's finely tuned palate must be able to discern, in his words, "the very top notes" of taste in ice cream. Daily, John tastes and evaluates an average of 60 samples of his company's six styles of ice cream. "Each morning my job is to taste all the previous day's ice cream that was produced," said John. "Number one, I do it early because that's when taste buds are most fresh. Secondly, all the ice cream that was produced the previous day is still in-house. If there's something wrong with it we can put it on hold." John is the number one flavor developer and spokesman for the company.

Quality is a key concept for John. The company has strict standards for its ice cream, which is called "premium." The chairman of the board has empowered each employee to "pull the plug" at any stage of manufacturing if quality standards are not met. "Our consumers should expect a good eating experience," said John. "Additionally, they must feel good about the value for their money, not only in flavor, taste, and texture, but in a consistently high quality product."

To maintain consistency in its ice cream, the company relies on the finely honed taste buds of its tasters. They approve any product or changes in a product before it goes out. Just to be considered for the position requires an extensive dairy background and top results on a rigorous sensory training exercise. Each plant has a "number one" taster and a back-up—colds or viruses adversely affect tasting ability. They must not smoke, of course. They also don't drink.

The tasting process itself has critical elements. Always present in the pocket of John's white lab coat is a gold plated spoon. These spoons are the mark of a true taster, since they have found that plastic, wood or other metals can impart a resinous flavor. To taste, John swirls a spoonful of ice cream around in his mouth tasting first for creaminess, then flavor, then sweetness. No, he doesn't swallow. Yes, like his peers in the wine business, he spits!

When asked about an interesting story during his 10 years as head taster and flavor developer, he came up with a spicy one. A few years ago, he worked on ice cream flavors that would appeal to Hispanic consumers. "I came up with a double strawberry, a good strong eggnog-type of vanilla and an excellent coconut pineapple. Another flavor was a jalapeño pepper ice cream. In reality, the jalapeño pepper was quite good, however, it was one of those rare ice creams that you could take the lid off and smell. Ice cream, because it's frozen, doesn't have a smell, so that sensation is unexpected. Also, when you taste ice cream, the first message your 9,000 taste buds get is that this product is cold. Now in this ice cream, the second message was 'hot.' It was the only food I've ever experienced that gave that double response immediately. It made my brain kind of jump up and down. We decided not to put jalapeño ice cream in the marketplace and fool mother nature. It tasted good though, we still have a reserve."

John's success is partly attributed to his heritage (he really does have ice cream in his veins, thanks to a long line of relatives in the business), but also to his philosophy on balance in life. "So many people get into a corporate arena and make themselves an island with all their weight behind their employment," John said. "That's wrong, that's out of balance. Balance includes spending time with your family, nurturing and encouraging them, and giving to the greater community through your time, your talent or your treasure." He practices what he preaches with two board memberships, church volunteering and the nurturing of five budding "tasters" at home.

Balance has one more special connotation for this "golden tongued" taster. "I use the word 'balance' in ice cream as well. You see, it is easy to slap a new flavor together—that's 90% of the job. But it's the last 10% of extra care, love and commitment that gives the fineness, the balance—That's quality."

Angle View 21
HOW TO RUN A BANK
Stephanie - Bank Branch Manager

Stephanie is a vice president and bank branch manager. She is responsible for managing the overall profitability of her branch, which includes keeping loss control within planned guidelines, exceeding sales goals, and enhancing the bank's image in the community. In addition, Stephanie must manage, motivate, and train bank personnel.

Stephanie has consistently been rated as one of the top branch managers for her bank. Her secret is simple. "I set high expectations for myself and then I do whatever is necessary to get the job done. I'll stay up late at night or get up early in the morning if necessary to work on reports or whatever." "Also," she went on, "I think it is important to be proactive. I try to plan, and strategize ahead of the program. I don't like being in the position of having to react when I could have used foresight to plan ahead. I'm totally committed to my job and I think the results show and speak for themselves."

She described how she personally strives for a quality performance in three of her key areas of responsibility: sales, community involvement and personnel management. "In sales I know I will be compared against a goal and against other branch managers. For me to feel good, I like to be on top of the report in the number one, two or three position. One of my strengths is in interacting with customers. My personality helps, but more important is my confidence and performance. I have a lot of confidence in myself when working with customers. I think my high confidence level rubs off on them and they in turn feel I will take care of their problems. As a result, I'm able to easily establish a rapport and I get a lot of referral business. I take good care of my customers. I follow up. I get the job done. They learn that."

"In the community, it is important for me to be well known," Stephanie continued. "I am an active member of the local Chamber of Commerce. Since my bank is located in a fairly small town, it is relatively easy to be known if you're willing to donate your time and effort. I try to be as involved as possible."

"In my third area, personnel management, I feel it is important that my employees are satisfied, that they enjoy their work, and that they get appropriate support and performance feedback. I feel that I communicate well with my employees. I try to encourage them to set their goals high. I do find, however, that certain aspects of personnel management are difficult. While I feel I have an eye for recognizing how to place people in positions that suit and challenge their talents, I still find it difficult to figure out how to push the right buttons so they are satisfied and motivated in their jobs. That's the hard part. You try to stroke but everybody has different buttons that need to be pushed; that's something I have to work on."

When asked about how things can get in the way of doing quality work, Stephanie talked about work overload. "Sometimes I find there's just too many things going on at once and I just don't know where to focus. I'm putting out fires and being pulled in too many directions. That's when I have to take a minute, sit down and prioritize my work. Part of the problem is I have a tendency to do too much myself. I have to delegate more."

Overall for Stephanie, doing a quality job necessitates keeping a positive attitude. She said she had to keep that outlook everyday because there are always obstacles to overcome. "I've learned after many years in the business that there's no unsolvable problem. It's important for me to have a positive and calm attitude. All day we are dealing with the public. We have to assure them we have every problem under control and there is always a solution. I think anyone seeking a quality performance record should take a very sound approach to problem solving. Keep positive and be confident in your personal ability to find solutions. Of course, it also means you must know your job well."

Another recommendation Stephanie has is for people to really access their weaknesses and be realistic about them. If there are deficiencies that would affect work performance, work toward strengthening and ultimately overcoming them. She also stressed that training and learning never stop for high performers, yet it's important to know when to distance yourself from your work and enjoy other pursuits. Lastly, she said, be committed to your job and set high expectations for yourself.

Angle View 22
NO MORE INNER CITY RIOTS?
Pat - Executive Director, Non-profit Agency

Pat is the executive director of a youth service bureau in a large city. She has been the overall administrator for this private, non-profit group for over seven years. The center serves "at risk" youth between the ages of 8 and 18 who, without programs like Pat's, can become victims of the economic and social problems facing kids in inner cities. The center focuses on crisis intervention for families in turmoil. It provides parenting education, employment programs for youth, and an after-school recreation and tutorial program. The overall premise is to keep families intact and assist those that are dysfunctional. Over 750 youth and parents are assisted each year by this program which has been in existence for over 23 years.

Pat's responsibilities are to design programs, oversee their implementation, handle public relations, negotiate contracts, raise funds and manage a paid staff of 22 employees. She has a budget in excess of $500,000 per year. To do a good, high quality job, Pat feels she must be able to concentrate and focus on what she is doing. Additionally, she feels it is important to have a very good line of communication with her staff. "Good communication is critical for me," said Pat. "I have three key program directors and I stay in touch with them daily. My staff looks to me for direction. It's important for them to have some kind of leadership. I provide them with a foundation. They don't need to feel like they are floating in the wind. When I design a program, everything is included, from staff requirements, how it is supposed to be run, etc.—it's all mapped out. Once I approve it and give it to them, it's hands off for me—it's up to them to run the project."

Pat's job of late has had special challenges and at least one unfortunate incident that had a profound effect on her outlook on work and life. First, economic times have affected funding, so fundraising has become an increasingly difficult challenge. Pat found she had to focus more of her energy on writing grant proposals and requests. That took her away from some of the program development responsibilities she enjoyed so much.

On a more critical level, 1990 was a pivotal year for Pat. Over the years there had been several burglaries at her agency, but on December 26 of that year, there was one that had a significant effect on Pat. "This particular break-in was personal," said Pat. "It saddened me and it had an effect on me that was unlike any other break-in or problem that occurred during the time I worked there. This time they only disturbed the things in my office. They rifled my desk and took my personal things—things like cassette tapes, tissues, and little pictures. They didn't take anything that belonged to anyone else, just my things. To compound matters, they took a fire extinguisher and sprayed everyone's office; that is, everyone's except mine. I can't tell you how many times I've thought about that incident and tried to figure out why someone would do that."

It was after that incident that Pat began to rethink her priorities in life. "I thrive when I have four or five things going on. I need to be very busy because I am a high energy type of person. However, that incident plus my going to school for my Ph.D. eventually knocked me out of balance. I truly thought I could juggle my professional, personal, and academic life - truly. Everything went crazy—my daughter broke her leg and the break-in was bothering me.

I really was sure I could work, go to school, deal with my husband, deal with my children, and deal with my house. I found I simply could not do it all. I would be the first to say this superwoman stuff doesn't work. For a long time I carried that shield, I did everything and thought I had everything in balance, but the end result is that you can get burned out—you hit a wall."

After some months had passed, Pat recognized the "wall" and took action. She dropped some of her college credits and took a short leave from her job. By recognizing that things were out of control and making changes, Pat once again gained control. The mark of a quality performer, in this case, can be described as one who knows when her high standards are being compromised. It is important to know when to put on the brakes, assess a situation, take action, and come back strong.

Pat will readily tell anyone how important it is to be able to take hold of your life and not let anything throw it out of balance. Another recommendation from Pat is to exercise regularly. She believes exercise is an important stress reliever. "My advice to others," Pat concluded, "is to first of all, take care of yourself, both emotionally and physically. You have to strike some kind of sane balance to do a quality job."

157

The Angle on Chapter 9

*The work
of the organization
must get done...however,
human beings are vital to all aspects
of the work. This chapter looks at adding
balance to the department, from the vision, mission,
and recruitment, all the way down to every individual's
daily activities. Take a preventive look at the
possible challenges to balance in
the workplace and learn how
to manage them
effectively.
RG*

9

HOW TO ADD BALANCE TO THE DEPARTMENT
Rick Griggs

There are many parts of balance theory with direct applications to traditional departments, including the current version of self-managed work teams. Balance in the department is not a luxury. The old guard may never admit that the authoritarian style of management is dead. People won't put up with an organization that intimidates, hastens disease, and finally kills them. No more! The new millennium not only brings drastically new demographics for the workforce but also a fundamental model shift away from hierarchical management and narrow focused "company" devotion, towards a fresh look at balanced individuals. We define balance as a "stable, calm state of the emotions—a satisfying arrangement marked by even distribution of elements—characterized by the display of symmetry" (Personal Wellness 1990).

INTERRUPTION BETWEEN WEEKENDS?

The evidence is mounting that these balanced individuals are the best assets money cannot buy. These folks drink less, smoke less, use fewer drugs, and miss less work. In other words, work is a well-managed priority in their lives. It is a critical milestone in their journey towards lifetime success and satisfaction. For too many others, work is a distasteful interruption between weekends. Smart management will wake up and "smell the balance" and then build it into the organization from mission statements and recruiting, all the way down to daily activities.

CONSISTENCY, VARIETY, MODERATION

The guiding trio of consistency, variety, and moderation applies as well to groups of people with common goals as it does to individuals trying to balance their lives. Whether it's the group manager of the self-managing team or the individual members, both can benefit by incorporating consistency of effort and direction towards the goals of the organization. When consistency is lost employees become confused and begin to squander their talents and motivational efforts. They don't know what to do. Without variety, people become stale and have difficulty maintaining intensity. The element of moderation is simply "burn-out prevention." This completes the circle where consistency makes up for the moderation. It's like the runner who knows that running too far, too fast will make her stop the whole program. But if she's moderate in each run yet consistent in running 3-4 times a week, it all balances out. Departmental moderation is countered by the consistent forward movement. Add variety and you get happy productive people.

In the pursuit of departmental balance, there are two initial difficulties. They fall into the areas of initial consensus confusion and gradual priority drift. Up front consensus is improved in an atmosphere where people meet regularly and trust that the interests of the organization take precedence over the interests of particular individuals, especially those in power. Consensus is rarely 100% but it builds with successive iterations. The reality is that you'll never convince some members of the department but if time and discussion are generously allowed, more and more will accept the "verdict." Discussions should be frequent and "open." Gripe sessions are the best thing a manager can hope for. Here's where you get communication and emotional unloading at one time. No progress is made until "gripes" are aired.

GRADUAL PRIORITY DRIFT

Gradual priority drift is when an individual or a group "drifts" away from carefully developed priorities. Since they are usually made on past information (including past or current successes or "failures") they always mold and melt as time passes. They mold to current urgencies and melt away when consistency is lacking. In the department situation the complexity is multiplied by the number of significant contributors. An example of gradual priority drift was when I was employed as training manager at Intel Corporation. I had a three shift operation with supervisors and skills trainers covering day, swing, and night shift. We trained the production operators who manufactured integrated circuits or "chips." My first action was to be personally trained and certified in several of the actual silicon wafer fabrication operations. Next, we jointly developed a mission, objectives, and guidelines for priorities that most of us agreed to, and could work with. Two months after my arrival, the plant manager asked me to add the document control department to my operation. Two more months passed and I was asked to take over a portion of the area's management and engineering training. These additions added two individuals to my staff. Team members couldn't understand why our meetings were less effective, and why priorities began to drift. It wasn't until we reviewed our mission and objectives that we were able to stop the drift and bring our priorities back into line with division goals.

WHERE ARE THE MARCHING ORDERS?

A mission statement is not a luxury, nor is it permanent. More and more workers are demanding to know the "why's" of their jobs and activities. A short and complete description of what the organization does and how it chooses to do it can work wonders in giving people motivation to remain on a course of action. When starting from scratch, get wide input in rough, unedited statements. Allow time to digest and assimilate various complementary and contradictory ideas. Now is also the time to add the notion that well-roundedness in life, will assist in accomplishing portions of the mission. It's a fearful shock to ask a group of 35 middle managers and supervisors in a fairly successful firm to discuss their mission, and only get blank stares and silence. It's equally frightening to then hear a litany of department specific statements that jealously guard individual fiefdoms with no regard for the larger success of the other co-workers in the same room. The consultant or facilitator gingerly backsteps to avoid the obvious embarrassment of the executives and leaders of the firm, and then moves into a quick exercise to begin formulating a cohesive statement of purpose.

Sub-groups should be able to look at the mission statement and pull their existence from it. They should also be able to get a sense for the method of achievement. Statements such as "We will crush the competition" and "We are a no-nonsense, results oriented machine" suggest an aggressive method of achievement. On the other hand, statements such as "Our well-rounded employees put nothing above customer satisfaction" and "We value and respect clients, employees, and associates" imply a much different organization.

ADDING VALUE TO THE DEPARTMENT

The organization does not exist for the individual employee, yet an outstanding method of accomplishing goals is to pretend that it does. Assuming clarity of vision and mature selection of strategies and markets, the employees' balanced personal life can be a major asset in reaching company or agency objectives.

Balance objectives bridge the gap between the mission and what people do on a daily basis. We've heard the term "lost in the translation" but perhaps never realized how much it is happening in our organizations. My estimate is that over 50% of all the time, energy, and effort is wasted in most organizations. This is because between arrival and departure people do good things that do not add value. Managers fix major crises that do not add clients. Executives attend urgent meetings that do not guarantee happy, repeat customers. My big fear is that the estimate of 50% may be too low.

BETTER TRANSLATOR HUBS

Improving the translation between the organizational mission and what people actually do between arrival and departure is the job of global success factors and specific objectives. These translator "hubs" are most effective when jointly developed, pulled directly from the mission, and succinctly stated. If a balanced and well-rounded workforce is an asset, the place to transmit this belief is right along with the other important departmental objectives. Among the six to 10 specific directional objectives, make room for one more that specifies the benefits to the department of employees who have a reasonable balance among work, family, personal, recreational, and health issues.

DO YOU RECRUIT OR CONVERT?

Select the best or select the balanced? Which will bring the most benefit to the organization? Recruiting drives usually begin with a careful analysis of the types of new employees that will best fit the needs of the group. This analysis is distilled from a list of experiences, skills, and attributes into a checklist for measuring potential candidates. Now is the time to add an item on balance.

Shrewd purchasing managers learned early that the lowest bid rarely means the best decision. Marketing managers know that the best looking , desktop published market report has nothing to do with the discipline and rigor used to answer the critical questions about market penetration in the current business environment. The bottom line is that eventual success includes looking at underlying issues and factors that interact with each other. The result is more a function of the underlying factors than the surface ones.

The nightmare of the bad hire lingers for too long. Although there are no guarantees, one predictor in getting solid people is life balance. Those who have done it will probably continue to do it. Most recruiters clearly understand that past behavior is always the best predictor of future behavior. If some type of balance fits into the group's mission, success factors, and departmental objectives, it should translate all the way into the selection and appraisal of personnel.

THE BALANCED JOB DESCRIPTION

If major values and strategic plans are in the mission and translated via the divisional or departmental objectives, the group is well above average. The cream of the crop recruit people who have demonstrated alignment and competence in the surface, as well as the underlying factors needed to compete in the industry and satisfy customers. The ultimate, practiced by a select few, is to imprint accurate action steps into the daily activities of every member of the group. By adding customer input and system re-evaluation the cycle has been completed. The only way to move above 50% productivity in any organization is to harness the individual talent and aim it directly at fresh missions and objectives.

Individual talent is better harnessed in an atmosphere of balance and equilibrium in life and work. Each of those individuals has a personal life (whether active or latent). The success of their personal life will directly impact the mission and objectives they are paid to support. Most often, managers and executives have a poor grasp of the updated mission and cannot translate the important parts to particular departments. This forces middle and line managers to work longer and "harder" themselves and demand it of everyone around them. They are trying to hit a moving and invisible target by overworking, spreading stress, and instilling fear. This fear takes the form of diminishing job security and increasing embarrassment.

SUBTLE DEMANDS TO OVERWORK

It's depressing to hear the tales of qualified engineers, managers, trainers, designers, and production line workers outlining how they are pressured to look like they are overworking and "committed" to the firm or agency. How ridiculous for organizations to desperately need productive output yet they instill a climate of pretense and outright fakery. If people want to do good work and departments need good work how does it get so messy?

After a session teaching professionals how to add balance to their lives, and still get the job done, a female engineer told me the following story. "I've usually completed my day's work by about 6 pm but I can never leave before 7 or 7:30. There's so much subtle pressure to forget your personal life and live at the office. I have a husband and two kids who hardly see me. Once I even got a "joking" electronic mail note from my boss saying he saw me leave around 6:30 pm—he asked was I slacking off and going home early?"

Another gentleman was born and raised in another culture. He came to the U.S. and got a good job that paid well. He said "I'm in a daze as soon as I walk in the door in the morning. There's so much to do and we never know which items are really important—it changes so fast. Then there's always the fear of not looking like you're working hard enough and maybe losing your job."

DEPARTMENT "TAG" TEAM

Remember the children's game of tag? Whoever was "it" had to chase the other kids around until they could catch another child and "tag" them. This would immediately relieve the first person of being "it" and transfer it to the new child who was just tagged. Today's tag team is where different members in the department join forces in an organized and educational fashion. During the process 80% of the emphasis is placed on the person acting as the teacher. The purpose is to convey the essential pieces of the job to the "new" person. After a day, week or even a month, both switch to the other position. Where the second person, whose job it is, takes 80% of the lead. The other 20% is designed to allow the follower to attend to his/her regular essential job functions and any non-delegated tasks needing attention. When the "tag" is made, both people move to the other position and switch roles for the same amount of time.

This type of "tag" serves to go beyond simple cross-training. The lead person should focus more on mission, objectives, philosophies and past experience. The past experience, in particular, weighs heavily in giving the second person a close feel for the actual decision making process and the skill that a person accumulates after being in a position for some time.

ORGANIZATIONAL "TAG" TEAM

Now is the time to switch positions with someone in another area of the organization. The benefits will be in exchanging ideas and big-picture information with the rest of the employees in the original department upon returning. Again, one position gets 80% of the attention in an effort to teach and demonstrate the essential background and functions of the position. When the "tag" or switch is made, the emphasis should still be on department-wide benefits that the two will offer to both departments. Many inter-department issues revolve around perceptions and assumptions. A large number of these perceptions and assumptions have never been tested or explored. This position exchange is similar to a process used in a negotiating course. The two parties are given a scenario, a negotiating process, and their starting positions. Each group rotates representatives at the "negotiating table" to attempt to settle the issue in the "win-win" fashion. This process unfailingly degenerates into near chaos until the facilitator announces that each party is to send a diplomat to meet in a strategy session with the opposing group. When they reconvene at the bargaining table, each party now has someone in the other group who understands the situation and has broken through some of the incorrect assumptions and perceptions. In nine out of ten class simulations, the conflict is resolved and the negotiation is completed soon after the diplomats return from the opposing team.

INDUSTRY "TAG" TEAM

This may be the biggest risk of all. It also takes the most planning and organization. Two people in different industries plan, in advance, to join each other on their jobs for 100% tag team exchange. The home group plans to allow the visitor full access to the strategic and tactical aspects of the job. Careful introductions are made to other employees to clearly explain the temporary visitor and the non-competitive nature of the exchange. I remember hearing someone at Stanford University say "I wish we could rotate people out into private industry for a while and then back into the university setting." We went on to discuss how people who remain in the same industry or the same organization for several years need the added exposure to calibrate their situation. The industrial "tag" would do just that.

Most consultants will agree that every group feels they are special and unique. Groups also think that their issues and complexities are more unique and difficult to untangle than others. Exposure to other groups can only help in expanding perspective and learning new tools. One drawback is the mistaken idea that this would be like some of the high technology companies that worked people to death for seven years and then offered them an eight week "sabbatical" for recuperating and putting their lives back together. Well, quite often the dazed employee slept for the first two weeks, then realizing the absurdity of killing themselves for another seven years, began

165

looking for a new job. Industrial tag should start before the seven year "daze" kicks in. The next step is to quickly apply the new tools and lessons to the home organization.

What are some of the possible blocks to adding balanced achievement to the organizational "tool box?" Here are some of the issues I have encountered in my own organization and in the many companies, agencies, and governments that have experimented with some form of professional balance.

EXCUSE FOR MISSED DEADLINE

Some people will use the excuse that by trying to balance their lives there wasn't room for getting a particular priority accomplished. They may say things like "I couldn't get that done in time because I was trying to keep balance in my life." Or "You do want us to stay balanced don't you? This would have thrown everything out of whack for me, and we know that's not good, is it?" Well, what's not good, is not getting the work done. There's nothing in the literature that says balance should be a substitute for achievement. In fact, they go hand in hand. It's a way of getting the achievement done quicker, cheaper, with more well-rounded support. Watch for people using this excuse. These will often be the same people missing other deadlines and using subtle excuses aimed at the particular hot buttons and values of the leader or manager. If the manager or other team member is into balance, they'll use balance as the excuse, if they are into thoroughness, then thoroughness will be the excuse, if the manager is a quality proponent, they'll use the excuse that they were only trying to do high quality work. To counter this, go back to the mission, success factors, and individual tasks to emphasize that the job responsibility must be met. Balance is an ingredient that adds to the effort and the outcome.

THESE PEOPLE ARE...LOSERS?

The people who appear to lead balanced lives seem, on the surface, to be in lower level positions within the organization. The subtle, yet false correlation between balance and low achievement is frightening to most achievement oriented fast-trackers. The connection between well-rounded family people and promotability is seldom made in some industries.

Part of the answer is to fix your measurement system so that it documents and rewards solid accomplishment rather than appearances and effort. Too many people rise to the top of the ranking list because they linger at the office until 7 pm and leave most of their electronic or voice mail messages at odd hours. I once heard a middle manager explain how she tried to differentiate herself from all the other would-be fast trackers by saving her voice and electronic mail massages and then sending them late in the evening or on Saturdays to give the impression that she was totally devoted to the organization. Unfortunately poor measurement systems and "out-of-town" managers only see this pseudo-effort and in their minds, up this person's ranking by a few notches. Look carefully at solid results. The surprise may be that the understated quiet ones are often be the best producers. Balanced people are not weaklings, nerds or losers.

NO "TOUCHY-FEELY" BULL

Upper management by their words, actions or inaction, wants faster action towards the "urgencies" they have created. Old style managers can't stomach any wasted time on this "touchy-feely" bull. The impression is that there is no connection to the bottom line. These folks remember what worked in the 70's and 80's and missed out on the transition that occurred in the 90's.

The response is to go back into the company's history and document the tragedies and crises that resulted from this short sighted "no-nonsense" style. Many high technology companies were founded by other people who left firms run by leaders who couldn't or wouldn't risk being vulnerable. This vulnerability, possessed by the greatest leaders, opens the door to increased employee resources, new products or services, and great expansions in market penetration. The short term approach has no "room" for balance. Many long term, fundamental assets are passed over when people can't see past their office door. If you want the job done well for enduring customer satisfaction, allow human beings the tools and freedom they need to perform. There are no absolute guarantees, but it will help.

HEY YOU MESSED UP! SOME EXAMPLE!

You are the catalyst for balance in your workplace yet you don't lead a 100% balanced life. People see flaws and missed opportunities and may conclude that if you preach this stuff and can't even do it yourself, then something's wrong. This usually results from the way you set yourself up. If you are one who always has to be right and espouses absolute perfection, even in minor, low priority areas, of course you can prepare to be nailed to the wall as soon as you show a weak part of your armor. The fact is you'll never be 100% balanced in your life or your department. You may move toward the goal and continually renew and reassess your approach to getting there. Every motivational speaker gets de-motivated at times, good writers put out some lousy paragraphs, and great painters put out pieces mistaken for elementary school art work. All may still be good speakers, writers, and painters.

SURE DON'T SEE ANY AT THE TOP!

The leader does not believe in this resource and, without necessarily being against it, simply doesn't support it. Sometimes he or she sets an example that is 180 degrees contrary to symmetry and equilibrium in work, family, personal, and community aspects of life. As the next chapter will discuss, these leaders may be obsessed or possessed and tend to spray this style on others, especially their top lieutenants. This is a big problem! It is also a common problem. This person at the top usually has reward power, legitimate power, coercive power, and other personal characteristics often mimicked—often feared by employees. You, as the change catalyst, must use the control you do have in your own area of influence. After assessing your true level of belief in contrast to that of the leadership of the organization, begin to build the balance asset into your work area. Let the results speak to the leaders. Down the road you can start to build the case that the results you had control over, not the capricious ones dealt by market changes and other outside forces, were influenced in some way by instilling balance through your recruiting, your purpose statement, success factors, and daily activities. Make your point that balance had a key and tangible role in your success.

IT'S FEMININE...IT'S WEAK

People get the impression that this "balance stuff" is feminine, weak and not traditionally business oriented. Fine, but let them know that this view is somewhat outdated. Doing what works and saving lives is not stupid, and only a fool would equate feminine with weak. Some of the roughest and toughest achievers in history made it a point to build well-roundedness into all of their important endeavors. They struggled to re-energize, re-charge, and build in supporting structures that carried them through tough times, through unexpected times. These were the smart people who knew that risk taking was really risk minimizing through planning. People who look like they are taking a lot are risks are actually reducing risks through alliances, diversifying, and by having contingency plans. This sounds a lot like a broad based effort towards bottom line results. This complaint or accusation reminds me when I was finishing up my masters thesis at the University of the Pacific in Stockton, California. I tried to stay physically fit by continuing my gymnastics routines I had performed in high school and college. The university's football team asked me to conduct some short sessions on flexibility and coordination. The coaches knew that these skills increase strength and assist in most physical activities. The team needed more than my short sessions to win but you sure wouldn't go up to one of those guys and call him feminine or weak because he learned a few "tour jetés."

I'LL LOSE CONTROL OF STAFF

You feel letting go of the corporate toughness will make you lose your edge. In informal studies 90% of respondents will say they lead unbalanced lives. If you ask several employees you will come up with similar numbers. Much of this is due to feeling controlled and compelled to work so much as to ruin other parts of their lives. The Japanese coined the term "karoshi" to signify death from overwork.

Too many managers and team leaders try to mask weak skills and poor missions and objectives with too much control. The thinking, whether conscious or not, is that they know what needs to happen and they are somehow blessed with the knowledge of the best ways to make it happen. They are usually wrong on both counts. The world moves too fast to keep up on all aspects. I remember a friend named Jim who was promoted to engineering manager in a highly successful firm. He loved the new job but lamented the fact that he could no longer keep up. His personal level of technical expertise had to be sacrificed in favor of managing the global corporate concerns of market planning, personnel management, and research and development. He wisely trusted his top people to ferret out the details of what needed to be done and how best to do it. He was very successful.

I've seen one case in the past 10 years where an employee took the trust and flexibility a balance-oriented manager gave her, and then abused it. Most of the time, giving control away is gaining the control you need. You want to lose control so that bright and motivated people take the ball and run with it. As long as you've clearly outlined which end of the field would be a touchdown, let them decide which route to take, and when to slow down, dodge, and speed up. They may want the touchdown as much as you!

10 WAYS TO ADD BALANCE AT WORK

1. CLEAR MISSION: This is the number one way to stop the habit of trying to carry water in a leaking sieve. No clear mission means that over 50% of the activities performed by the group are wasted. It's hard to spend too much time molding, clarifying, and communicating the mission.

2. VISIBLE OBJECTIVES: These are the factors that translate or connect the big vision of the organization into seeable and doable chunks that people can get excited about. This helps them "own" the vision or mission, and maximizes the use of their talents. An added bonus is that visible objectives help harness that "5 pm motivation" that is often reserved for baseball, bowling or the after work aerobics class.

3. SELF-MANAGING TEAMS: Form teams around customer issues. Provide the teams with the best tools and training available. Assist the teams in developing methods of measurement and accountability so that success can be recognized. Finally, allow the teams the flexibility that human beings need to flourish.

4. FLOW CHARTS: The activity of flow charting the path of products or services towards the customer can spot duplication and

opportunities for strategic combinations. Don't make the mistake of flow charting the traditional flow of activities. How you did it in the past may have no connection with what your real customers want today.

5. ELIMINATE: Get rid of it. Test the current need for reports, memos, meetings, print-outs, visits, etc. Ask what would be thrown out in budget cuts or emergencies? What no longer adds value or progress towards the mission or objectives? These items should go. They're dropped cold when someone gets sick or suddenly leaves the organization. Why wait?

6. SIMPLIFY: Simplicity makes room for balance. Overdone elegance and perfection only serve to add stress to groups often hanging on by a thread. Simplicity allows time for family, personal time, sports, hobbies, and health. All of these benefit the well-run organization.

7. REWARD PREVENTION: Never give rewards or recognition at the expense of preventing the crisis in the first place. Prevention is usually hidden. It requires time to spot it and to understand the "bullet" you just dodged. It helps if you have good measurements and accountability so you can spot prevention. Well-rounded people tend to have keen awareness and perspective in this area.

8. REWARD BALANCE: Reward balance in the context of achievement. Balance alone is not the goal of the organization. The end result is achievement. Like the other ingredients of success (preparation, training, tools, communication, motivation, etc.) attention and recognition will increase its occurrence. Good measurement systems will highlight the correlation between balance and the end result or achievement.

9. STUDY ACHIEVEMENT: Other people and groups have done something similar to what you are trying to accomplish. There is always a better way to do what you are doing. Seek out and study the principles of achievement. They are found in biographies, annual reports, seminars, and open discussions.

10. TRUST: When individuals and departments genuinely dedicate themselves to an issue or a cause, magical events begin to occur. When people persevere and re-dedicate themselves, the universe mysteriously comes to their aid and sits in their corner of the ring.

Throwing hours or dollars at a problem is the easy way out. Marshaling productivity and balance lead to sustained progress.

NO TRUST...NO GLORY!

In the early 80's my job was to provide productivity improvement programs to specific departments at National Semiconductor Corporation. All my training and common sense told me that in order to be effective, you must gain the trust of all levels of an organization. To do this I spent many late evenings with the swing and night shift production operators. My days were spent with management and day shift, so as to round out my visibility and familiarity with the entire department. As they began to trust me, story after story unfolded in the quiet corners of the "clean rooms." These are the futuristic enclaves where "bunny suited" production workers carry out the silicon wafer manufacturing operations dictated by management and engineering. I got shivers when a production worker told me about the abuse and condescension they endured from a couple of arrogant engineers. Eighteen months prior, they had a special run of experimental wafers. A "boat" of 18-20 of them would be specially tagged for extra care and attention. The engineer in this case gave no information, bullied the workers, and humiliated them so that he could keep complete control. Late one evening they had had enough. They took the "prized" lot and emptied it behind one of the large multi-million dollar machines. Extensive searching never solved the mystery of the missing silicon wafers. My feeling was chagrin and puzzlement at being the first person these workers felt comfortable enough with to tell the story. It could have gotten them fired on the spot. I worked on solving the root causes of the unfortunate symptoms. And no, I didn't breach the trust these workers put in me.

PEOPLE WANT TO PERFORM

When you demonstrate trust and expand the scope of what people do, you magnify their ownership of the organization's purpose. I've heard employees say they love working for an enterprise that respects their whole life and has its act together with clear goals. Many of them say that the reduction in stress and the addition of balance is worth from $5,000 to $15,000 in annual salary, not to mention the life saving benefits.

Everyone is motivated. Most people want to do good work. If you don't believe this, take the most "unmotivated" employee you have ever met and watch the magical transformation that occurs at 5:05 pm when they grab their baseball bat, bowling ball or aerobics gear and head out to do what they really want to do. Someone who was half asleep and moving in slow motion 10 minutes ago suddenly walks and talks like they just won the lottery. Why is this? The answer is two-fold, first they have a choice in these activities and second, they are, in some way rewarded handsomely for participating. They choose their after work activities and they get some "major strokes" for their involvement. The same thing can, and should happen on the job.

POINTS TO REMEMBER/THINGS TO DO

1. Recognize and reward consistency, variety, and moderation.
2. Recruit, hire, and train for balanced achievement.
3. Eliminate the fear of job loss and embarrassment that demands overwork on non-mission issues.
4. Remember the game of "tag." Use it for continuous learning within your department and with other industries.
5. Beware of excuses and evasions as you attempt to use balance as a bottom line asset.
6. Review and apply the 10 ways to add balance to your team.
7. Trust must be nurtured. It builds slowly and gradually. Without it you'll be a present-day example of King Tantalus.
8. Whenever possible offer people choices and useful rewards.

Department Balance Inventory

Compare employee, supervisor, manager, and team leader scores.
1 = Never, 2 = Rarely, 3 = Sometimes, 4 = Often, 5 = Always

1. The organization encourages people to be balanced.
1   2   3   4   5

2. Our department encourages members to be balanced.
1   2   3   4   5

3. Throughout the organization it's generally okay to have personal and family priorities.
1   2   3   4   5

4. We limit the amount and duration of "extreme" efforts where people are forced out of equilibrium.
1   2   3   4   5

5. We list and discuss a reasonable group of well defined priorities.
1   2   3   4   5

6. We adjust plans and priorities often enough to keep them useful and valid.
1   2   3   4   5

7. We anticipate and plan ahead for most contingencies.
1   2   3   4   5

8. Professional development and learning are openly encouraged and rewarded.
1   2   3   4   5

9. On-going training and development are priorities.
1   2   3   4   5

10. Well-rounded people are considered valuable assets.
1   2   3   4   5

10-20 = Deep Trouble   31-40 = Path to Success
21-30 = Trouble Ahead   41-50 = Excellent Balance

(Permission granted to copy this form after purchase of book)

Angle View 23
SHE MIXES QUALITY, FUN & BALANCE
Barbara - Telecommunications Company Quality Expert

Barbara is a quality manager in the purest sense. In her position with a multi-billion dollar telecommunications company, she has the responsibility to investigate service oriented companies that have been nationally recognized for high achievement in the area of quality service. "My goal," Barbara says, "is to learn other companies' methodologies and philosophies so I can impart that knowledge to appropriate areas within my organization. This information will help improve my company's ability to identify and set quality standards, both internally and externally."

Even though a search for quality techniques is part of her job, Barbara sees a clear distinction when it comes to her personal goals of quality performance. "I know I'm successful when I'm *value added*. That is, when there is more of a benefit for my customers to use my services rather than trying to do something themselves. My customers are the various lines of business within my company. I must be responsive and provide answers and results in such a way that pleases them."

To provide quality service, Barbara said three elements must be present in a job. First, you must understand how your job fits in with the scheme of things. You cannot be working in an "information vacuum." Second, you have to feel empowered to make decisions. The third element is, you must understand what is expected from you by your customer and your boss. She stressed, "You have to ask. You do not want to operate under false premises."

Barbara is fortunate. She has those elements in her job. "Because I have such a supportive environment, I am in a position to perform at a high level and I work hard to do just that. To keep competitive I use my creativity and my organizational skills. I set goals and then I get the results I want in a cost effective manner. For example, I wanted to arrange for a group from my firm to visit another firm that had received the Malcolm Baldrige award for quality."

"Now, one way would have been to arrange for my associates to visit the company's home office since they had a tour program for interested visitors. While a relatively easy solution, I'm always

175

digging deeper to find the best, not the easiest. I went an extra step and found a way for my co-workers to visit their local operations and actually get a more in-depth and personal analysis. To make the experience even more focused, I briefed my co-workers in advance and planned an agenda that would be sure to address their key concerns."

"The approach worked. My company representatives, in this case my customers, were extremely pleased and learned a great deal more than a simple trip to the home office would have provided. This, for me, is doing a quality job. It means going that extra step and taking creative risks."

When asked about keeping the equilibrium in her life, Barbara had these thoughts. "I think I do a good job because I keep it in proper perspective. I make time for those other things in my life that mean a lot to me, such as graduate school, volunteer work, and the people I care about. I like my job, and could do it every hour of the day, but it would totally unbalance my life. For me, balance is having a job I like, but also placing a high value on the things I want to do. I feel having my whole life in balance makes work more fun."

Angle View 24
FROM DESKTOPS TO MAINFRAMES
Leyla - Product Marketing Manager

Leyla works for a California Silicon Valley software company. Her company designs and manufactures the software that installs on desktop and mainframe computers to provide the networking that will allow a variety of computer systems to interface or "talk" with each other.

Leyla, who has a BS in electrical engineering and an MS in systems management, is a product marketing manager for one of her company's highest revenue product lines. Her responsibilities are to track and monitor her software product from the design and production process, through customer service and sales training, to ensure the product maintains its high standards and meets the consumers' needs. To do this requires interfacing with a variety of areas including engineering, manufacturing, packaging and customer service within her company. "There's an incredible amount of matrix management going on," Leyla said. "I have a high level of responsibility within the company but really not that much authority. I'm responsible for the entire success of the product which means I have to drive everyone in the company to do what I need done. Some of them are in other states and some are here in California. It's pretty challenging to try to pull all those people together."

High quality work for Leyla would first of all mean having a product without any errors. In the software business, that can be virtually impossible, because as Leyla admits, any software program is susceptible to bugs. "One of my biggest responsibilities concerning quality is to ensure that the test process in engineering is as thorough as possible." Leyla continued, "Quality control is paramount for us. Also critical is how we handle our customers. Technical support is another big issue. We must respond promptly when called and resolve problems quickly. Additionally, visibility in the field is important to do a quality job. Since I also do sales training, I must be visible and knowledgeable when it comes to my product."

One factor that affected quality for the workers of her company was a recent merger with another company. Leyla recalled a 6 to 12 month transition where employees had low morale due to

177

considerable ambiguity about which projects would be kept, eliminated or downgraded. Leyla said, "Mergers are really tough on companies. One of my motivators is seeing the reward at the end of a project—a quality product, happy users, the sense of fulfilling a need. When you're not sure that end is coming, it's real hard to be motivated and put in the type of concentration and hours that are required. It's very difficult. In the end, the merger was good for us, but the transition was very tough."

Personally, Leyla says that it is her nature to not do things halfheartedly. She approaches her job the way she approaches life. She gives her all, keeping in mind the need to balance quality and quantity. "I have to know the trade off's. There is only so much time to get things done. I have to be able to juggle a bunch of responsibilities, so I try to do a quality job—fulfill my duties, but I have to know where to draw the line. I have to know when a job is good enough. That is a difficult skill to maintain, especially for a job as varied as mine."

Balancing work and play is one of Leyla's keys to success on the job. In addition, she recommends keeping in mind that salary is not really enough of a reward to keep people motivated. She feels you have to have a sense of ownership; a sense of pride in what you do. "Also," she says, "be flexible because people set in their ways who don't make an effort to get along with people have a hard time doing a quality job because so often jobs require using the resources of the people around you." "Lastly, we all have those things we don't like to do. Each morning, do one or two of them. By the end of the week, not only will you have done the big and enjoyable jobs, but some of those dreaded jobs will be out of the way as well."

Angle View 25
"ANY WAY TO MAKE YOU HAPPY?"
Jennifer - Sales Representative, Athletic Club

Jennifer is a membership sales representative for a major athletic club. Her job is to attract new members and help them get comfortable with the services of the club.

For Jennifer, doing a quality job involves having the right kind of personal touch. She acknowledges that selling skills can be learned, but will admit that in her job personality, attitude and understanding are what put her a cut above the rest. "My personality is number one," said Jennifer, "I think for the most part people buy me and then they buy the club. I'm happy about the club, I'm happy about fitness and what it does for me. I sell that. I sell my own peace of mind and fitness."

Jennifer never aspired to a sales career, but, as many do, fell into her position quite by accident. Jennifer was an employee of an athletic club and was slated to move to a soon-to-open sister club as a manager. While reviewing the inside construction of the new club with her boss, Jennifer happened to answer a phone that rang with sales inquiries. The way she handled the calls prompted her boss to instead offer her a sales position in the new club.

One could call this a natural fit for Jennifer, who exudes energy and confidence. "I like people. I like making people happy and I'm motivated by seeing people smile. In sales, you probably have to have 75% personality and 25% empirical skills, plus a good product. There's no canned speech for everyone; you have to personalize each conversation."

Jennifer continued, "In my job there are two critical elements. First, learn to not just hear, but really listen to exactly what a client says. Find out what their needs are. Second, ask the right questions."

According to Jennifer, people seeking athletic clubs often have very different motivations. "Some people want an escape from a home situation. Some want to be able to get out of the office a few minutes each day, some want to lose ten pounds, some want to master a certain sport and on and on. I try to discover their desires and personalize our conversation. People want to buy what they want to buy."

"I know my job is to satisfy people's needs. That includes fitness needs and financial needs. I must always be at my best to do a good job. That means I must leave my personal stuff out of the office. It also means I have to know when to step back, take a few breaths and center myself to keep myself in control. A few breaths, putting a call on hold, or spending a few minutes alone in my office, all keep me balanced. This extra time, now and then, allows me to bring an uncluttered mind and a fresh approach to each situation or conversation. I can't be creative when I'm bogged down."

Sales has its down side, of course. Every potential sale won't be made. Every call won't be answered. Jennifer has the following approach. "You have to understand that you start with a NO. You have to create a YES. But in my case, usually they come to me, so I feel they intrinsically want to say yes. They may not know entirely what they want—once again, it's up to me to pinpoint their needs and encourage that yes to come out."

That philosophy rings true for Jennifer daily. One memorable case occurred before the club actually opened. Jennifer recalls when a "high powered" attorney called "His conversation started with a tirade berating athletic clubs, sales people, fitness and the like. Finally, Jennifer broke in and said, "Sir, is there any way I can make you happy this morning?" His anger was over a recent divorce, being grossly overweight, and out of control in every part of his life except his career. Jennifer's question, she later learned, brought him to tears. She said, "Had I been defensive I would not have established a relationship. I just had a sense he needed to yell at someone and get it out of his system. Not only did he join, but ultimately so did his ex-wife, his girlfriend and tons of his friends. It's his second home now and he's my pal."

"I have to be positive," said Jennifer. "I have to remember to pat myself on the back for small accomplishments. Things like, not snapping at somebody, listening two minutes longer, and making six people really feel good today. I also feel making lists is important. Write down what you do best, what you love yourself for, what you need to work on. Then every hour, every day, every month, chip away at those things needing improvement. If you make quality tantamount to success, then quality has to be the end, and success will come. If you focus on money, you'll (your success will) be short lived."

The Angle on Chapter 10

*Here's
where we come
full circle, back to King Tantalus.
But first we'll take a look at obsessed,
possessed, and "blessed" achievement. This not
only covers your personal issues, but companies
and agencies can be obsessed, possessed
or "balanced" in the way they go about
developing, manufacturing, marketing,
and distributing their products
and services.*
RG

10

OBSESSED, POSSESSED & "BLESSED" ACHIEVERS
Rick Griggs

In the early eighties I learned a hard lesson through another person's tragedy. After finishing my studies in psychology and business, I entered the world of high technology consulting. Two glaring facts stunned me. One, most people were working themselves into health problems and two, there were precious few role models and mentors. Of course, there were examples of how to get ahead as fast as possible, but I didn't see any long term approaches to productivity, customer service, and quality improvement that my life experiences and academic training showed were effective.

It was unfortunate that I had to witness a co-worker come to work early one morning, to get more work done, and then die of a heart attack that afternoon. I then made a career commitment to teach balance and achievement. This co-worker would work late and come in before dawn to reach a standard of perfection that she thought was needed. That perfection standard wasn't needed—she died between her desk and the waiting ambulance outside of the building.

This final chapter of <u>Quality Angles</u> will offer more on the "Tantalus"" Complex, but first it will give you a panoramic view of three types of achievement in your effort to reach the right levels of personal and work quality. Obsessed, possessed, and blessed (or balanced) achievement divide the quest for accomplishment into a) an unhealthy but conscious drive, b) an even more unhealthy and unconscious drive, and c) a well-rounded and healthy method of producing quality products, services, and lifestyles.

SOME DEFINITIONS

The dictionary links <u>obsession</u> with evil spirits and fixed ideas. The definition also covers compulsive and unreasonable thoughts and emotions. In another section it describes being <u>possessed</u> with images of the super-natural and again being dominated with fixed ideas. Let's take a closer look as we bend the definitions just a bit to highlight two dangerous levels of achievement.

The quality of your work life, home life, and family life can be affected by each of the definitions on the next few pages. Each of them determines how people go about their personal search for accomplishment and satisfaction in life.

OBSESSED?

<u>Obsessed Achievement</u> - Definition: The conscious, unrelenting pursuit of higher and higher standards of performance for yourself, your family, and your colleagues/co-workers. This is a purposeful decision to pursue goals in a way that puts other important life issues on hold. The person makes a conscious decision to sacrifice camaraderie, free time, hobbies, family or other opportunities to get something done. Examples of obsessed achievement would include the decision to write a book, make a movie, finish a computer program, become athletic or win an election **while knowing** it would have negative effects on other parts of work and life.

182

Characterized by: Obsessed achievers are <u>always trying</u> to attain some goal of perfection in accomplishment. This conscious, relentless effort dictates most major and minor activities in the person's day-to-day life. They are aware of the obsession but do not change.

POSSESSED?

Possessed Achievement - Definition: The uncontrolled and unconscious pursuit of achievement to the extent of fanaticism. The tendency to automatically overwork and over achieve, in work, family, and in personal pursuits. Here, we have an unconscious pattern of pursuing goals in a way that puts other important life issues on hold. The possessed achiever works and lives in ways that sacrifice friends, work objectives, personal issues, family and health for reasons that usually cannot be explained. They have lost sight of what they were trying so hard to accomplish in the first place. Examples of possessed achievement include working from 6 am to 7 pm everyday, taking 7 aerobics classes a week, or requiring perfect departmental documents even when hand-written would suffice, without clear-cut reasons for doing any of them.

Characterized by: Deteriorating mental and physical health and an unrealistic grasp of reality. This unconscious, driven pattern often affects other family members and co-workers first, before taking its toll on the individual. They are unaware of the possession and do not change until a major event forces the awareness and then the motivation to change.

"BLESSED?"

"Blessed" or Balanced Achievement - Definition: The long term approach to lifetime accomplishment and satisfaction. This "blessed" approach combines the synergistic effects of a balanced lifestyle <u>and</u> full application of the many factors of achievement. Finally, we come to the well-rounded strategy of attacking goals in ways that respect and enhance other important life issues. These achievers pay regular, consistent attention to friends, work objectives, personal issues, family, and health. They have clear sight of what they are attempting to accomplish with everyone around them. These folks know the definition of quality includes conformance to specification, so they take the time to hammer out the expectations from others and of themselves. Sounds like they know a lot about <u>appropriate standards</u>! Examples of balanced achievement include setting reasonable work hours, exercising moderately, reading consistently, and varying personal and family activities.

Characterized by: The display of symmetry and a calm, stable state of emotions—a satisfying arrangement with an even mixture of elements. They are aware of some of the synergistic elements of well-rounded accomplishment but totally unaware of others. Their tendency is to build good habits, turn on the "auto-pilot" to keep them going, and then move on to other moderate objectives.

PERSONAL LIFESTYLES

Personally, you may notice a bit of yourself in each of the three types of achievement. Seminar audiences will distribute themselves rather predictably among the three types. During an interactive presentation, younger people or those in faster track careers will describe themselves as obsessed or possessed. It's interesting that most people in the care giving industries will also select these two. Other folks, older in age or in calmer and established industries, will select the balanced or "blessed" option more often. Without a doubt, someone will ask "can I pick all three?" The answer, although developed later in the presentation, is a resounding yes. Most of us bounce between categories once in a while, but spend most of our time in one. If anyone asked 10-15 people who know them well, they would probably get confirmation on which one they most resemble—obsessed, possessed or blessed.

You'll also notice that there are a few good things in each of the **obsessed** and **possessed** areas. Many reward systems mistakenly measure activities that fall into the first two categories. This gives people a clear hint that in order to make it in this or that setting you had better look obsessed or possessed. The benefits may be raises, bonuses, awards, trips, feature articles, social prestige, and a trophy spouse or lover. You may start by faking it because you really do value your personal hobbies and your family, and you'd enjoy living long enough to spend the money you're desperately trying to earn. The eventual result is that after spending a lot of time in any category whether or not you subscribe to its characteristics or values, you will become that category. The young innocent teenager who hangs around with gang members will undoubtedly take on the characteristics of those folks whether or not she or he initially believed in them.

Obsessed Personal Achievement is a continual preoccupation with trying to do it all. Do you see a trend to the items listed? Which ones would you circle as reflecting your life?
1. I try to have quality time with family.
2. I always work hard and play hard.
3. I can do anything or have anything.
4. I won't be stopped or slowed down.
5. I get a thrill from getting things done.
6. I focus on always improving.

Possessed Personal Achievement is a dangerous state of unawareness. You've reached the level of the patient who no longer feels the pain because the disease has eaten away the pain receptors. Circle the ones you agree with.
1. I don't need to change anything.
2. I don't feel any need for quality time.
3. I'm unaware of anything else my family needs.
4. My co-workers don't need anything else of me.
5. I'm unaware of anything wrong with my body.
6. I can't figure out why I'm tired and angry.

Balanced Personal Achievement doesn't just happen. After the repetition and diligent application of the many factors of achievement, you gradually learn a natural lifestyle where the "default" mode is on the good, healthy, and balanced side. Without much ado, you find yourself being and doing what you personally need for satisfaction and accomplishment. Check the list below. Are you balanced?
1. My lifestyle is varied and moderate.
2. Most of the time I naturally eat well .
3. It's normal to feel some stress.
4. I usually sleep well.
5. I generally exercise consistently.
6. I socialize regularly with friends and acquaintances.

IS DARELL BALANCED?

Darell went to college and then continued on to get his master's degree. It wasn't easy, with a new wife and tight finances. Although he did well in his course work and spent the necessary time to continue that trend, he also took time to develop close relationships with other students and some of the faculty. He knew how important a healthy body would be to his mental sharpness and the everyday strains of family (kids in the future) and work life. He took up bicycling and after flirting with obsession, in the form of a 120 mile bicycle trek from college to Yosemite National park with a friend, pulled it back into a balanced form of healthy exercise and recreation.

Darell graduated and excelled in his first job. He later switched companies and made a strategic move to Oregon where he and his wife started their family near other family members. Darell added prestigious jobs to his resume while continuing to bicycle and raise his family. He and his wife Jan celebrated their 17th wedding anniversary amid class reunions, two children, and a well-balanced lifestyle. Sure, he pops into the first two categories once in a while, but guess where he spends most of his time?

Let's shift gears and shine a light on what happens within agencies and various organizations where people come together with presumably share similar interests and objectives. The following section introduces how the three styles of achievement play out in groups of people.

ORGANIZATIONAL LIFESTYLES

Much research has been done to confirm that groups can and will take on a distinct personality based on time together and experiences shared. Individual styles and values are often tossed aside in favor of the emerging group personality. The tragic experience with the religious group in Waco Texas dramatically showed how an individual member's personal style and beliefs can be set aside in favor of the attitudes and opinions of the group. The beliefs held by the group in Waco were so cohesive and unified that they violently held law enforcement officials at bay for nearly two months. Groups can transform individuals into an entirely different entity.

Groups of people working towards common goals can fall into the same three categories of achievement we just explored. You'll notice a few similarities where the characteristics of the possessed individual for instance, will match those of the possessed organization. You'll also see where the group has the power to transform each style into something altogether different.

WHO SPRAYED ME?

A major factor common to the organization is that anyone in a leadership position will "spray" the organization with their particular, personal achievement style. In other words, the catalyst for the organizational style will usually be the style of the founder, president or top manager.

Obsessed Organizational Achievement can be spotted by a continual barrage of short-lived motivational programs that beg and beseech unskilled and untooled employees to dig the organization out of the mess it's in. This department or government agency tries hard to get the results without laying a proper foundation.
  1. We gave 120% last quarter; now let's give 140%.
  2. If we try harder, we meet more objectives.
  3. We always have new motivational programs.
  4. If something doesn't work, we scrap it.
  5. We are trying hard to win.
  6. Beat the competition.

Possessed Organizational Achievement often results from early, phenomenal success or an individual leader who expects narrowly focused goals to be met on a short term basis. This unhealthy group can be quite successful in finance, marketing, investments, and publicity, but grinds people up at a dizzying rate.
  1. Those who can't cut it should leave...now!
  2. Quarterly numbers tell the whole story.
  3. Over promising and under delivering is common.
  4. Our quality must be perfect...always.
  5. We will win!
  6. Kill the competition.

Balanced Organizational Achievement is marked by groups that provide the tools, the skills, and the environment that human beings need to perform over the long haul. Since balanced

187

employees perform better and longer, this organization trusts that the investment in people will be paid back handsomely. The quality of personal and work performance is enhanced.

1. We lay the groundwork well in advance.
2. Open discussions at all levels are common.
3. Winning is the result of the right actions.
4. We re-charge batteries and sharpen tools.
5. Continuous education pays broad dividends.
6. We are the competition.

TAKING AND GIVING OFFENSE

There is another difference between the obsessed and the possessed methods of reaching goals and living life. The obsessed person **takes offense** and the possessed person **gives offense**. Here is an examples of what I mean. I met a music instructor who was using a fancy electronic device to tune instruments for a beginning class. Someone asked if that gadget was the replacement for a manual type of tuning device (the tuning fork). Without thinking, she defensively snapped back "You try tuning several instruments without this gadget!" Although she quickly backed off and showed a very pleasant personality, the initial reaction was to take offense that someone would question her efforts to get several instruments tuned, after a hectic class, and no one to assist. She was consciously trying very hard to do a good job. The obsession created a narrow focus where a friendly effort to chat was perceived as a threat. It is common for the obsessed achiever to take offense at idle verbal comments, confusing body language, and unclear written feedback. The possessed person is oblivious to these perceptions and merrily goes along bothering many people around him/her. In both cases, they're so wrapped up they've lost a clear view of the horizon, they can't see that others are just trying to help, make conversation, or just don't know how to deal with them when they're in the obsessed or possessed frame of mind.

MYTHICAL IMAGINATION

Let's go back to King Tantalus. You remember the King we discussed at the beginning of these chapters? To genuinely understand how the "Tantalus" Complex affects work teams and individuals, let's explore some pieces of Classical Mythology.

Zeus, the god of gods, was responsible for sending many mythological figures through the underworld kingdom of Hades, via the three judges, to a deeper infernal region called Tartarus. The lucky ones, being judged more favorable, were sent to the Elysian Fields (the most famous street in Paris bears this name). A group of the not-so-lucky, called the "damned," were sent to Tartarus (I've lived in cities that *should* bear this name). The "damned," sent to Tartarus, included Sisyphus- condemned to roll a rock up a hill because he finked on Zeus, Ixion- tied to a burning wheel because he tried to rape Zeus' wife Hera, The Danaids- 50 daughters of Danaus condemned to vainly draw water through a leaking sieve for killing their husbands, and King Tantalus- son of Zeus and Pluto sent to the underworld for revealing the secrets of the gods. In each case, the damned suffered eternal humiliation and punishment for their sometimes heroic, sometimes stupid acts.

WE LEARN FROM MYTHS

It's humorous and enlightening to learn about the crazy deeds and consequences throughout the pages of mythology. But the lessons involved carry serious weight. Joseph Campbell spent a lifetime collecting and interpreting the myths of the ages and, rather convincingly, argues their credibility and contemporary application. Many others agree that myths serve to explain the unexplained and to guide us in making moral and spiritual decisions. The myths tell us of sailors trying to pass through the narrow strait between Scylla, the six-headed monster on one side, and the swirling gulf of Charybdis on the other. Too close to either meant certain death. The stories of Odysseus, Jason, and Aeneas include the "struggle of choices" between Scylla and Charybdis. Myths teach us that this "struggle of choices" is an everlasting dilemma for humankind.

THE MEANING OF LIFE & CIRCE'S ADVICE TO GLAUCUS

Throughout the ages, humankind has struggled to interpret the Universe. We all look for signs or guidance—for the guidelines or parameters of the epochs in an attempt to identify our place in history, and ultimately, to know how to live our place in history. Myths gently tap us on the shoulder and let fly a colorful, flaming arrow, illuminating a path we should explore. When that direction is explored, the mortal has a better understanding of where they fit within the ages of time and how best to live their allotted portion on the earth, in other words, their personal meaning of life.

Myths are filled with nudges towards the meaning of life and work. Odysseus, for example, after having originated the great Trojan Horse swindle (where he hid soldiers inside a huge wooden horse) and winning the Trojan war, spent 10 years trying to return home. Homer's Odyssey describes the difficulties, choices, and transformations involved in his success. In crossing the threshold of the new millennium, the story still speaks to us and guides us today. Other myths give advice with a romantic slant. Circe, the sorceress had a nasty practice of turning those who looked upon her into swine. In a rare, good mood she admonishes Glaucus, one of her victims, "You had better pursue a willing object; You are worthy to be sought, instead of having to seek in vain."

The mythical story of King Tantalus spells out the cause and effect nature of the universe with one of the effects of misdeeds being a perpetual and "tantalizing" quest towards our goals. Each time King Tantalus bends to drink he is reminded of his past actions that now cause him to move towards the refreshing water but never to consummate the quest. Looking upwards to the ripened fruit on the low hanging branches, he again reaches, and again that cursed gust of wind awakens and snaps the branches just out of his reach. Would this mythological figure know that his predicament would add a new word to future dictionaries? Could he have guessed that around the year 2000 A.D. individuals and work teams would continue to replicate his style of moving towards and away from their aims with the same futile and repeated actions?

HE WAS A VICTIM...WE AREN'T

Shortly before completing this chapter, I met a woman named Eryn, who gently quizzed me about the direct application of a story from Classical Mythology to the 21st century real world. I was stunned that someone not only knew of the story, but could quickly analyze it and even poke a few holes. She made a good point in that King Tantalus was a victim, and by Zeus' order, could not change his situation. She wondered if the mythical tale applied to us, since he was a victim and we aren't. The "Tantalus" Complex puts the responsibility for getting there, and staying there, squarely on the individual or team. The instructional value in borrowing from the classics may require a few liberties. It also opens up contextual critique and logical broadsides to the metaphors. So be it. He was a thirsty, hungry victim. We have a option not to put ourselves in the same damned place.

IMAGINE THIS!

If we allow our mythical imagination to instruct us we will surely see more clearly. We would hear the distant voice of King Tantalus. He is reminding us to remove the endlessly tantalizing portion of our personal and career quests by "sniffing" around for good quality examples. He's fed up with being "tantalized." He would tell us that "Someone or some group is out there doing it right—go find them and learn." He might pause to look at his reflection in that damned water and shout "Get off your butt and learn how to lead...learn about empowering people and how going out on a limb can save you." Let's not fool ourselves, he's not be up to speed with the previous chapters dealing with the fancy ideas of diversity and Total Quality Management, and he certainly would never have heard of quality in television and broadcast media. In his grizzled, weary state, he would think they were crazy imaginings of that "idiot" Zeus, whose fault it was anyway, that he was stuck here.

His anger aside, you can bet he would agree with learning the basics of measurement, equality, and continuous improvement. Many centuries ago, when he was free and proudly ruled his kingdom, he always favored preventive and proactive thinking that avoids going backwards. He didn't, however, always practice them. Ambivalently flattered and suspicious at having a "complex" named after him, the King might advise us to be careful of those three levels of the complex—minor, major, and tragic contradiction. "Never sweat the small stuff—that minor contradiction" he would continue, "In my day, I knew how to live and enjoy life and work. If you focus here you'll go crazy." "On the other end," we can imagine him adding, "Keep your hands off the tragic contradictions until you get professional help."

A reflective pause suggests he is contemplating telling you some enchanting story of his knights or messengers biting off too much in some Golden Fleece or Holy Grail type of story. But all he says is

"The tragic level of this complex will only get worse if avoided or approached by amateurs." Changing his mind, he tells the story, "I remember two princes and a queen in my kingdom who should be here in Tartarus, like me. They fiddled around with tragic problems for too long before getting the prophet Tiresius, the solemn ruler Odin, and other professionals involved." Snorting and coughing a dry, thirsty cough, he adds "My clearest wisdom and ageless experience tell me that the middle level or major contradiction, is where most subjects—Oh, excuse me—people, can do the most good."

After several swipes at ripe mangoes and juicy pomegranates, the circular ripples slowly expand away from his chest. King Tantalus looks down, and with old age and eternal sorrow etched into his face says, "The balance part is good—it will keep your head clear and your progress on track. Please come back and visit again...there's much more to learn"

POINTS TO REMEMBER/THINGS TO DO

1. Everyone is a little obsessed, possessed, and "blessed."
2. We spend most of our time in one of the three areas.
3. Organizations can be obsessed, possessed, and "blessed."
4. Improvement at the organizational level affects many people.
5. Myths in general serve a useful purpose in explaining human life.
6. Specific mythical "stories" convey high-value and time-tested advice.
7. It's okay to allow your "mythical imagination" to guide you and your team.
8. Don't be a victim like King Tantalus, use your energies, intellect, and choices to avoid the trap of the "Tantalus" Complex.

"Tantalus" Complex Inventory

"Tantalus" Complex: "Moving towards and away from goals at the same time due to faulty methods of living, working, and of approaching the goal."

GOAL #1 _____

Movement Towards Goal #1

_____

_____

Movement away from # 1 _____ % away =

Movement away from # 1 _____ % away =

#1 TOTAL % WASTED EFFORT = ____

GOAL #2 _____

Movement Towards Goal #2

_____

_____

Movement away from # 2 _____ % away =

Movement away from # 2 _____ % away =

#2 TOTAL % WASTED EFFORT = ____

GOAL #3 _____

Movement Towards Goal #3

_____

_____

Movement away from # 3 _____ % away =

Movement away from # 3 _____ % away =

#3 TOTAL % WASTED EFFORT = ____

(Permission granted to copy this form after purchase of book)

APPENDIX A

60 ANGLE VIEW RECOMMENDATIONS

Each of the 25 Angle Views included in the book offers good information. Their interviews were recorded, written, edited, and re-written. Other exciting people were interviewed, but for reasons of space and editing, we could not use all that they had to say.

Appendix A includes many of the recommendations listed by those included and some that were not. We hope you'll find more helpful information for you personally and for your team. We have added to some of them and also included a few of our own.

1. You've got to be into people. No matter how hard you try, I don't think you will reach your highest level if you are not able to work with your customers and staff. You must relate to them, encourage them, and be there for them.

2. Understand your customer and cater to your customer. When it comes to judging the quality of what you do, the customer is really the only one whose judgment counts.

3. Be prepared. Know everything about your job that you can humanly know. Take the time to study and research so you will be confident and competent.

4. Be very honest. People can always spot a fake. Speak what is in your heart. Be gentle, but speaking the truth is usually the best way to go.

5. Be deeply entrenched in your marketplace. Understand your business and your customers. This requires lots of time and patience but it's always worth it.

6. As much as possible, be very organized. No one gets very far by being unorganized and inefficient. You may think it takes extra time that you don't have, but it will take more time later.

7. Prepare well. People have the idea about luck putting them in the right place at the right time. If you're not prepared to take on the opportunity that may confront you, don't expect to succeed.

8. Treat people the way you would like to be treated. It's the old Golden Rule. You may get help from sources you never expected.

9. You need to sit down and determine whether or not you like what you are doing. If you don't like your job, you should get out and do something else. Find the courage to find something you love!

10. You need to be able to know how you can make a meaningful contribution to your organization, You have to control the assets around you. You have to harness the power to get the job done.

11. Don't be afraid to empower your people. Know their skills and find ways to best utilize their strengths. If you don't do this someone else will.

12. Have a positive attitude—enjoy life. If you take yourself too seriously it'll harm you in the long run. Step back and look at the big picture.

13. Do only what you really want to do. Nothing else will inspire you and motivate you do continually do your best. This will also make it easier for you to stay motivated.

14. Seek positive people and pick their brains—ask questions. Hang around people with a positive attitude and a healthy outlook on life. Stay away from the negative people.

15. You have to understand how your job fits in with the scheme. Where does your work go and who needs to use it next. If you lose sight of this you might as well start looking for another job.

16. You have to feel empowered to make decisions. Don't sit around and wait for someone else to give it to you. Like they say, if your ship hasn't come in yet...swim out to meet it!

17. You have to understand what is expected from you by your customer and your boss. You have to ask. You do not want to operate under false premises.

18. You have to be committed. There's no way around this one. Good things only come to those who are really committed to something.

19. You have to be a good planner. It's hard but you have to slow down and take some time to plan. You'll never have enough time to do it, so stop making excuses and just do it.

20. You can't allow yourself to be distracted from the execution. Chance favors action and vice versa. One act is worth ten thousand words.

21. You need to be personally balanced. Don't let anyone take this away from you. Also, don't be intimidated by people pretending to work hard.

22. You need to be able to challenge yourself. You have to believe that even when people think you may not be able to do something (for example, those with a physical handicap) you can, and will find a way.

23. Think of your job responsibilities as being within a circle. Don't be afraid to "bump" that circle and take on new duties that expand your job. Soon your job will be bigger and more powerful. Your circle, hence your value to the company, will grow.

24. You need to find a support system for yourself. Include family and friends. This is like an investment in you and your goals.

25. You must remember to never stop learning and never stop teaching. You can learn from all experiences. Every time you teach someone, it helps you keep abreast of what you know and you may find someone willing to teach you something in turn.

26. Make a plan and keep nurturing it. You have to have a goal and then you have to believe in it and build on it. With this attitude it will happen.

27. Get to work on time and have your projects ready on time. The best excuses are really not excuses at all. Whatever reputation you get in this area will stick.

28. Listen carefully to the public (or whoever your customer is). They're telling you what they plan to buy and how they will decide on buying it.

29. Provide good service. Service can make up for a lot of things. People remember the little things as well as the big ones.

30. Be flexible. Things rarely go as smoothly as planned. Take a deep breath and change plans if you need to.

31. You have to enjoy what you are doing. That's the main reason I do what I do.

32. Take pride in your work. You are what you do to a certain extent because you spend a majority of your time doing it or working toward it.

33. Think positively, know you can do what you set out to do. Your attitude determines how far you will go.

34. Balance your life. It's been said before, but this is the part that most people overlook.

35. Don't listen to other people—listen to yourself. Trust your own gut feelings and intuitions.

36. Make a list of your attributes. Read it and get into thinking you're great. It may feel strange at first or that you shouldn't be doing this but it's okay.

37. Stay away from negative people and negative situations. Sometimes this even means family members or some of your co-workers.

38. Don't watch TV.

39. Get out into nature, walk on the beach, put your feet in the water, and learn to appreciate the simple act of breathing. Enjoy the fresh air.

40. Put out 100%. I used to think I was working much harder than others until I looked around and realized that I needed to get much more intense.

41. Shoot for your goals. Break them down into little goals and gradually you'll build up to bigger goals. Just don't play around with them and treat them like passing wishes.

42. If you have low self-esteem, look at someone who has achieved greatness in your field and pattern yourself after him or her. Learn about the problems they overcame.

43. Don't look at the negatives, look at the positive side of things if you want to be successful. You've got to deal with problems but don't dwell on them.

44. Listen to motivational tapes. Try to complete at least one side of the tape a day Apply the ideas and suggestions to your own drive for excellence.

45. One of the things really lacking is sensitivity. Be sensitive to your customers' needs as well as to those of your employees.

46. Have the proper motivation. If you don't like your job, don't expect to excel in it. One of the hardest things is to excel in something you dislike.

47. Don't fear living on the edge. It might be necessary to try something you really want to do. Teach yourself to push beyond your usual limits.

48. Find out in your heart what you want to do and start stepping in that direction. Big or small steps are OK—just don't stand still.

49. Encourage and compliment people who deserve it. Something you say can make their day. They might remember and cherish it for years.

50. Do something you enjoy and even if that thing seems incredibly crazy, there must be a way to turn that passion into an income. Make a list of what you like to do and don't like to do. Focus on the top two or three items you enjoy.

51. Practice concentration. Learn how to relax and clear your mind so you can think clearly and focus on your goals. This is a skill you can get better and better at performing.

52. Establish realistic goals and even write them down. Be clearly focused on what you want. Read and re-read the things you want to accomplish.

53. If you are a manager, be receptive to surround yourself with people who are motivated towards goals and willing to make daily strides to get there. Don't be afraid to hire or promote someone smarter or better than you are.

54. Be willing to listen and pay attention to what's going on around you. Filter what you can personally use in your own position. No one should be so self-confident that they can't listen and learn.

55. Find a profession you can say you really enjoy. It's three times as hard to do a good job when you don't like what you're doing. You can always see who likes their work.

56. Make it a point to recognize others for their good contributions. People won't keep trying if they never get the credit. Be honest and open about it.

57. Follow through quickly and completely with commitments. This is another of those reputations that will stick with you for years to come.

58. Keep a good sense of humor. Read the funnies or go to comedy shows to keep yourself laughing. They say that humor is the best medicine Use it daily!

59. Aim high. If you expect the best, you'll give your best. That's what pulls a lot of athletes and top executives through. Don't be surprised if you get what you aim for.

60. Plan well. It's been said over and over, but here it is again. It is true that "proper prior planning prevents poor performance." Make lists of your projects for each day.

APPENDIX B

QUALITY ANGLES GLOSSARY

Acceptable Quality Level (AQL)—Pre-determined levels of product quality or the number and level of defects that will be accepted and still considered to be good performance.

Appraisal—The inspection of the results of individual or group performance (product, service or activity) after it has been started, in progress or completed.

Baseline Data—Performance measurement taken before trying a new method or technique. This is the information collected in advance of starting a new program or improvement effort.

Commitment—The motivation and desire to continue acting on beliefs, opinions, and responsibilities. Usually considered to be one of the essential elements for individuals and teams to perform up to, and exceed expectations.

Communication—The process of sending a message through selected channels to a receiver and then getting feedback to check for mutual understanding.

Competence—The self-assurance of knowing how to do something well. It is based on education and experience.

Conformance to Specification—Formal definition for Quality. Sometimes listed as conforming to customer expectations.

Corrective Action—The process of correcting problems when the preventive approach is not used or does not work. This is the most expensive way to remedy problem situations.

Cost of Conformance—Cost of assuring that things are done right. Includes the early phases of prevention and appraisal.

Cost of Non-Conformance—The cost of doing things wrong. Includes internal & external failures.

Cost of Quality-—Cost of conformance + cost of non-conformance equals the Cost of Quality.

Customers—Those inside and outside an organization who depend on the output of individual and group efforts.

Error Cause Removal (ECR)—A program where employees list problems interfering with good quality performance. Management then assigns the appropriate group or person to fix the problem.

Failure—Internal failures are problems (non-conformance) found before going to the customer. External failures are found at the client's location or in the field.

Goals—Specific milestones or objectives that you, your family, your department or your organization wish to accomplish.

Management—Getting results through people by planning, organizing, directing, staffing, and controlling.

Measurement—A record of past performance used to influence future performance. Usually in the form of quantity, quality, cost, time or accuracy.

Non-Conformance—Not meeting the specified requirements. The opposite of conforming to specifications.

Organizational Goals—Stated, written or implied levels of accomplishment by groups of people with common aims and presumably a similar direction.

P-A-S Options—Three levels of standards (Perfection, Average, Stretch) used to gear performance to the appropriate level of co-worker needs and customer expectations.

Perfection Standards—Measures used to see if performance matches customer requirements or agreed upon expectations.

Personal Quality Standards—Quality measures for personal life based on values, opinions, and individual goals.

Planning—Outlining necessary requirements in advance for the accomplishment of goals—this is part of the preventive approach to overall quality.

PONC—Price of non-conformance. What it costs when you don't meet customer expectations.

Prevention—Anticipating and eliminating potential errors before they occur. Although often neglected, this area offers more opportunity for improvement than crisis correction.

Preventive Approach—Avoiding problems before they occur. This leads to better products and services at lower costs. It is much less expensive to prevent rather than correct problems.

Productivity—The ratio between inputs (labor, time, capital, energy) and the end product or outputs (widgets, services, completed product). Productivity can be increased either by reducing the input or increasing the output.

Q-MATCh—The acid test for professional and personal quality. Quality = Meets Agreed Terms and Changes. The test can be easily memorized and applied.

Quality—Conformance to specifications or requirements. Quality does not mean the "goodness" of a project, your job or a service.

Quality Awareness—The general awareness of quality principles and their effects on the organization or agency.

Quality Control—The process of ensuring the conformance to the designated requirements of a product or service. Often referred to as a department.

Quality Education—Knowledge, skills, and practices aimed at preventing, recognizing, and correcting poor quality performance. This relates to both before and after problems occur.

Quality Groups—A constantly emerging and adapting idea of groups usually made of teams of 6-12 people from an organization who study and apply quality improvement principles to work problems.

Requirements—All attributes, utilities, features, and benefits the customer expects to receive with the product or service. Your customer may be your boss, a co-worker or another department.

Rework—Doing something at least one extra time due to non-conformance to requirements.

Statistical Quality Control—The use of statistical techniques for active control during the manufacturing or development process. Makes use of real-time data for decision making. Also called statistical process control (SPC).

Trend Chart—Historical data shown in a graphical format. Usually in the form of line or bar graphs.

Zero Defects—The idea that perfection is the goal and no defects should be tolerated.

APPENDIX C

PROFESSIONAL BALANCE GLOSSARY

Here are some of the terms that have evolved during our work on balanced achievement and Professional Balance since we began in the early 1980's. Some of the terms will be familiar and are used with more specific emphasis or application. Other terms will be new. These were created and refined during the evolution of the Professional Balance process.

Achievement—The continuing process of selecting, strategizing, and accomplishing goals and objectives. Sometimes broadened to include the values and beliefs a person or group has selected for alignment with life and work.

Balance—The display of equilibrium and symmetry in life and work. Also, a calm, stable state of emotions supported by a well-rounded set of defined priorities that have been distilled and tested for accuracy and life, work alignment.

Balanced Achievement—A synergism with the specific end result of lifetime, sustained accomplishment. Balance is a means to the end result. The many factors that lead to achievement are enhanced with the use of balance. This is one of the major tenets of the Professional Balance program.

Careerstyle—The purposeful combination of professional career activities with personal lifestyle values and activities. This deliberate attempt to add <u>career</u> + <u>lifestyle</u> gradually becomes more natural and relaxed. The merging of values and beliefs with one's life work becomes a powerful tool in building a satisfying and productive "Careerstyle" that can lead to lifetime results.

Control Circles—A new addition to the Macro Balance assessment tool (see next page for the definition of Macro Balance). They are similar to the horizontal lines on control charts added to show upper and lower limits. Control Circles look like two circles, one inside the other. The space between the concentric circles signifies that the individual or team balance is within specification.

King Tantalus—In Classical Mythology varying accounts describe him as the son of Zeus and Pluto, husband of Euryanassa, and father of Pelops, Niobe, and Broteas. Three possible offenses brought him death and eternal damnation in Hades—The ancient tales depict him revealing the food and drink of the gods (ambrosia and nectar) to mortals, attempting to feed his dismembered son to the gods at a banquet on Mount Sipylus, and lying about a stolen gold mastiff. Condemned to join the other "damned" in Hades, some accounts have Tantalus standing in water, others place him in a tree. Each time he tries to drink, the water recedes and whenever he reaches for the ripe fruit, wind blows the branches out of reach. Added to his misery, is an enormous stone above his head forever threatening to crush his skull—(Origin of the word "tantalizing").

Macro Balance—A personal, partner or group priority development and assessment tool used to first identify and narrow priorities to a manageable level. Second, the tool assists in scoring each life priority, and finally, computing the total "out of balance" points reflective of the person's current life and work style. The process introduces control circles.

Micro Balance—Following the Macro Balance assessment, this continues with the dissection and analysis of the priorities with the most "out of balance" points or the biggest problem areas making symmetry and equilibrium difficult in the person's life, the couple's relationship or the department's activities.

Obsessed, Possessed, Blessed—Three unique methods that individuals and organizations use to handle stress and attempt to achieve goals and objectives.

-**Obsessed** achievers are conscious of the effort and continually try to reach more goals. They affect themselves first before others notice.

-**Possessed** achievers are unconscious of the set of patterns that run their lives. They exhibit signs of fanaticism and have a poor grasp of reality. They affect others without feeling the effects themselves.

-"**Blessed**" achievers are the balanced achievers. They handle their problems and challenges with symmetry and equilibrium in their work and their personal lives. They are well-rounded and, in the presence of accurate measuring systems, always excel.

"Ooption"—A whimsical reminder that it's okay to make mistakes. Once in a while, you have to say "oops,"—it's an option and a right that every human deserves. Mistakes do not equal failure but rather, can be building blocks to a well-functioning lifestyle and "Careerstyle."

Profile-Scans—A group consensus building and problem solving tool that collects and refines individual input concerning a team issue. The trademarked session takes about one hour.

"Tantalus" Complex—Loosely adapted from the Classical Mythology tale of King Tantalus, it is the self-defeating process of moving towards and away from goals at the same time. Individuals or groups select methods of getting to their desired ends that, in fact, do specific harm to that goal. Like King Tantalus in mythology (where we get the word "tantalizing"), we bend to drink and the water recedes, we reach to pick the fruit and wind blows it out of reach, in our case, because of our own contradictory actions and activities.

Translator "hubs"—These are the links between the vision of the organization and the tactical details performed by its employees. The translation takes the form of 8-12 broad success factors followed by specific objectives that tie individual, detailed activities to the larger mission of the organization.

BOOKS AVAILABLE FROM MANFIT PRESS

QUALITY ANGLES
& THE "TANTALUS" COMPLEX
Griggs & Carroll, Edwards, Gorham, Swartz, Warren
Manfit Press - hardcover, 206 pp.
$25.00

PROFESSIONAL BALANCE
THE CAREERSTYLE APPROACH TO
BALANCED ACHIEVEMENT
Rick Griggs - Manfit Press - hardcover, 209 pp.
$25.00

PERSONAL WELLNESS
ACHIEVING BALANCE FOR HEALTHY LIVING
Rick Griggs - Crisp Publications - softcover, 104 pp.
$9.00

QUALITY AT WORK
A PERSONAL GUIDE TO
PROFESSIONAL STANDARDS
Diana Bonet & Rick Griggs - Crisp Publications - softcover, 88 pp.
$9.00

HARDCOVER QUANTITY DISCOUNTS
1-10 = $25,   11-20 = $20,   21-50 = $15,
over 50 = 50% discount

SOFTCOVER QUANTITY DISCOUNTS
1-10 = $9,   over 10 = $7

Copy, then mail or fax order form on next page

BOOK ORDER FORM

For your convenience, please copy this form to order books from Manfit Press. Note the quantity discounts on the previous page. Remember, you can also order these books from your bookstore or ask your librarian about adding Manfit Press titles to your library.

Name:_____
Title:_____
Organization:_____
Address:_____
_____
Phone & Fax _____

Please send the following books

Title	**Quantity**	**Price**
QUALITY ANGLES		
PROFESSIONAL BALANCE		
PERSONAL WELLNESS		
QUALITY AT WORK		

HARDCOVER SHIPPING- $3. first book, $1.50 per extra title.
SOFTCOVER SHIPPING- $2. first book, $1. per extra title.

TOTAL SHIPPING $_____

P.O.# OR TOTAL AMOUNT ENCLOSED $_____

CALL IN ORDERS: 510/866-0793

COPY THIS FORM AND MAIL OR FAX TO:
MANFIT PRESS
P.O. Box 2390
San Ramon, CA   94583
Fax 510/866-0827

"TANTALUS BUSTERS"
GRIGGS ACHIEVEMENT TRAINING

- BEYOND STRESS MANAGEMENT
- COMMUNICATION SKILLS
- EFFECTIVE WRITING SKILLS
- EMPOWERMENT THROUGH ASSERTIVENESS
- FRESH LOOK AT QUALITY
- LEADERSHIP AFTER 2000
- MANAGING CHANGE
- PRESENTATION SKILLS
- PRESSURE PRESENTATIONS (advanced)
- PROBLEM SOLVING & DECISION MAKING
- PROFESSIONAL BALANCE
- SEXUAL HARASSMENT PREVENTION
- SUCCESS WITH DIFFICULT EMPLOYEES
- TIME & PRIORITY MANAGEMENT
- UNDERSTANDING & MANAGING DIVERSITY

NEW PROGRAMS!
- IMPROVING MEMORY SKILLS
- INTRODUCTION TO TELECOMMUTING
- ORGANIZING YOUR DESK & WORKSPACE

CALL: 510/866-0793

**FOR MORE INFORMATION COPY THIS PAGE
AND CIRCLE SELECTIONS**

**MAIL OR FAX TO:
GRIGGS ACHIEVEMENT + MANFIT PRESS
P.O. Box 2390
San Ramon, CA 94583
Fax 510/866-0827**

Name:_____
Title:_____
Organization:_____
Address:_____
_____
Phone & Fax _____